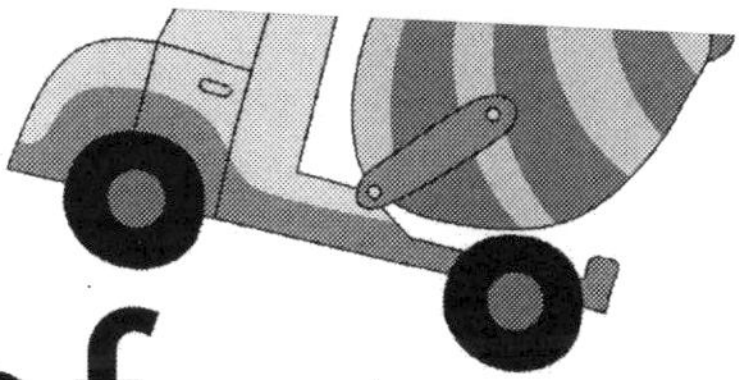

Big Book of TRUCKS Coloring Book

100 Coloring Pages!

Blue Wave Press

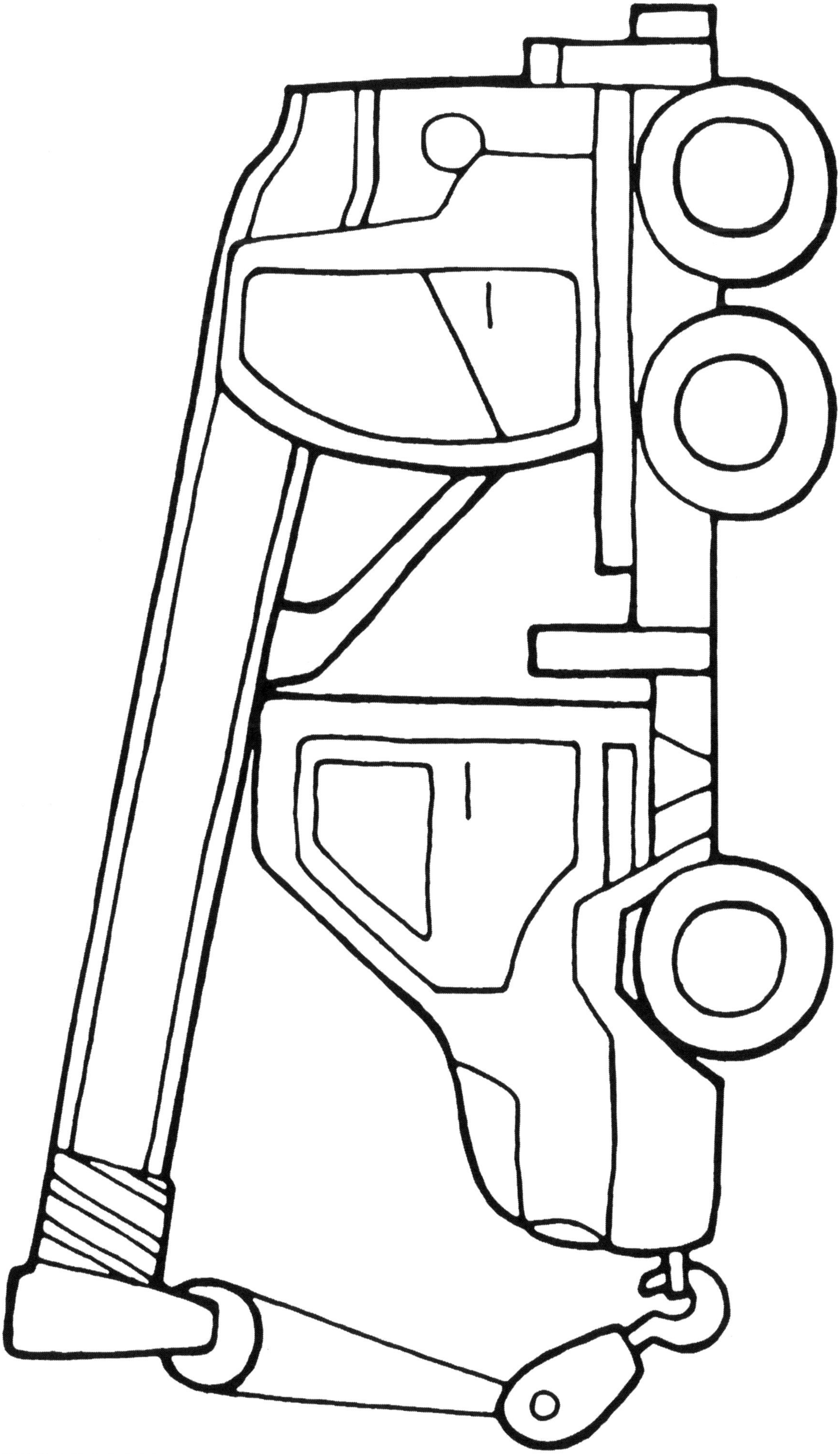

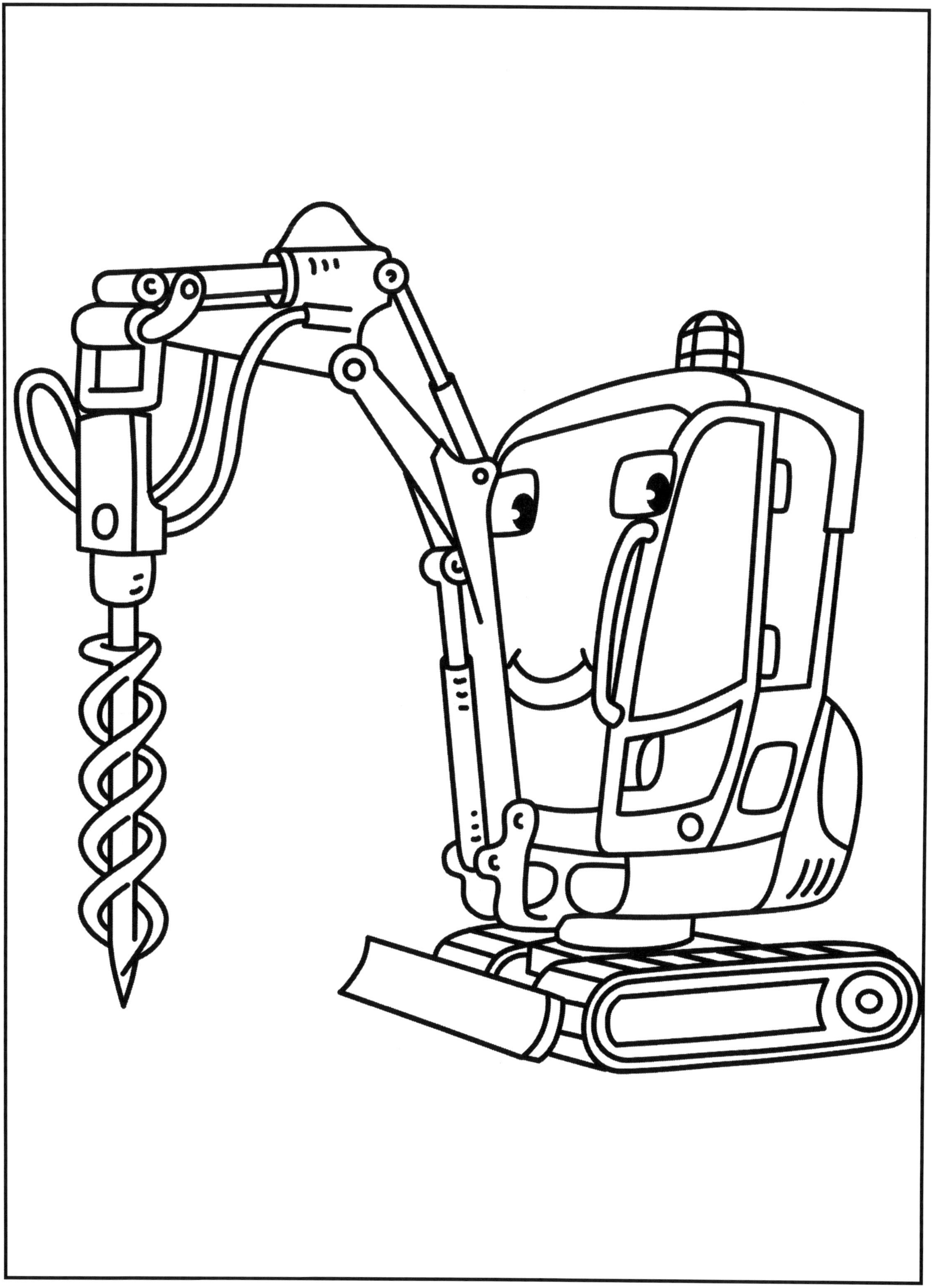

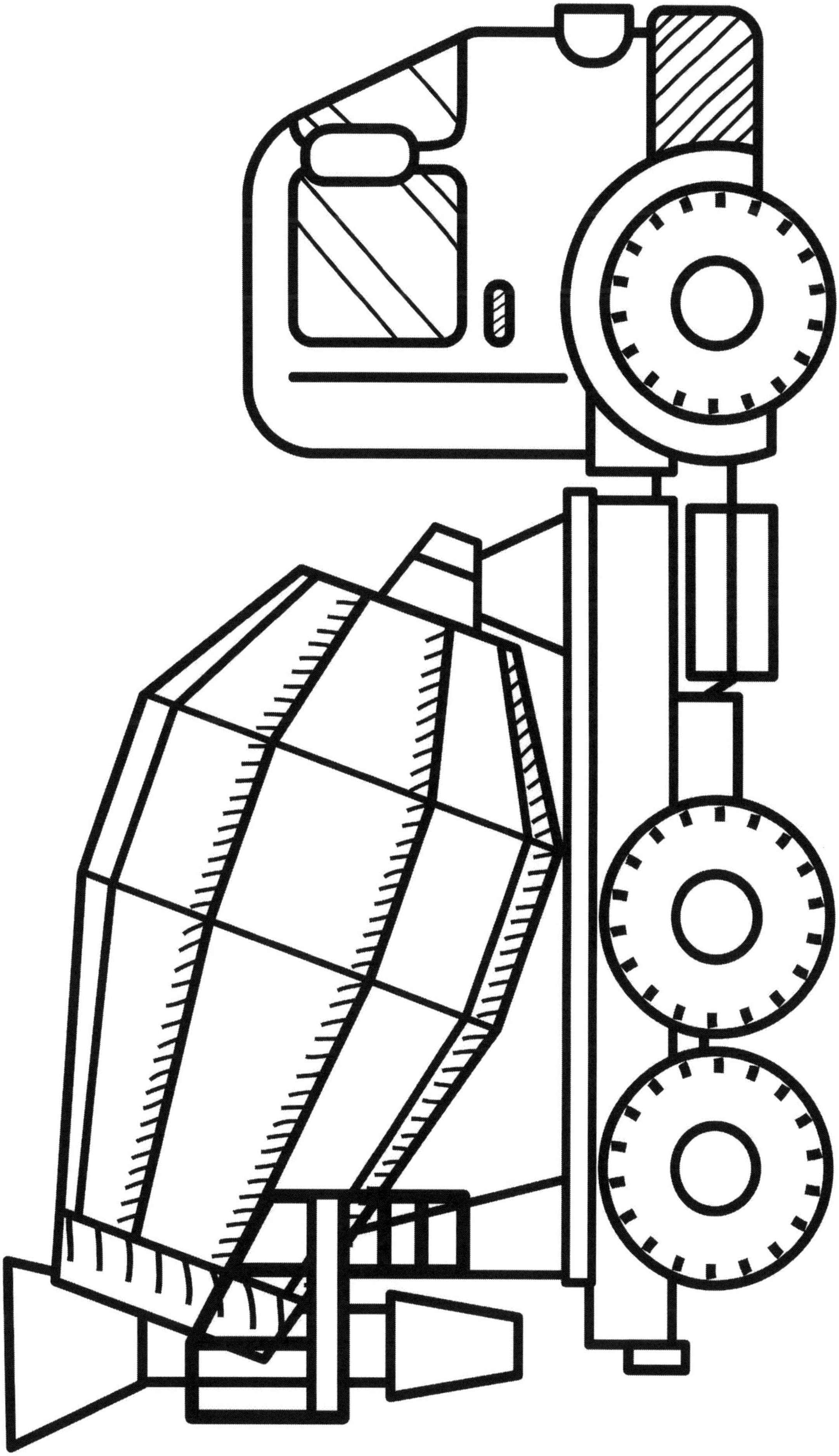

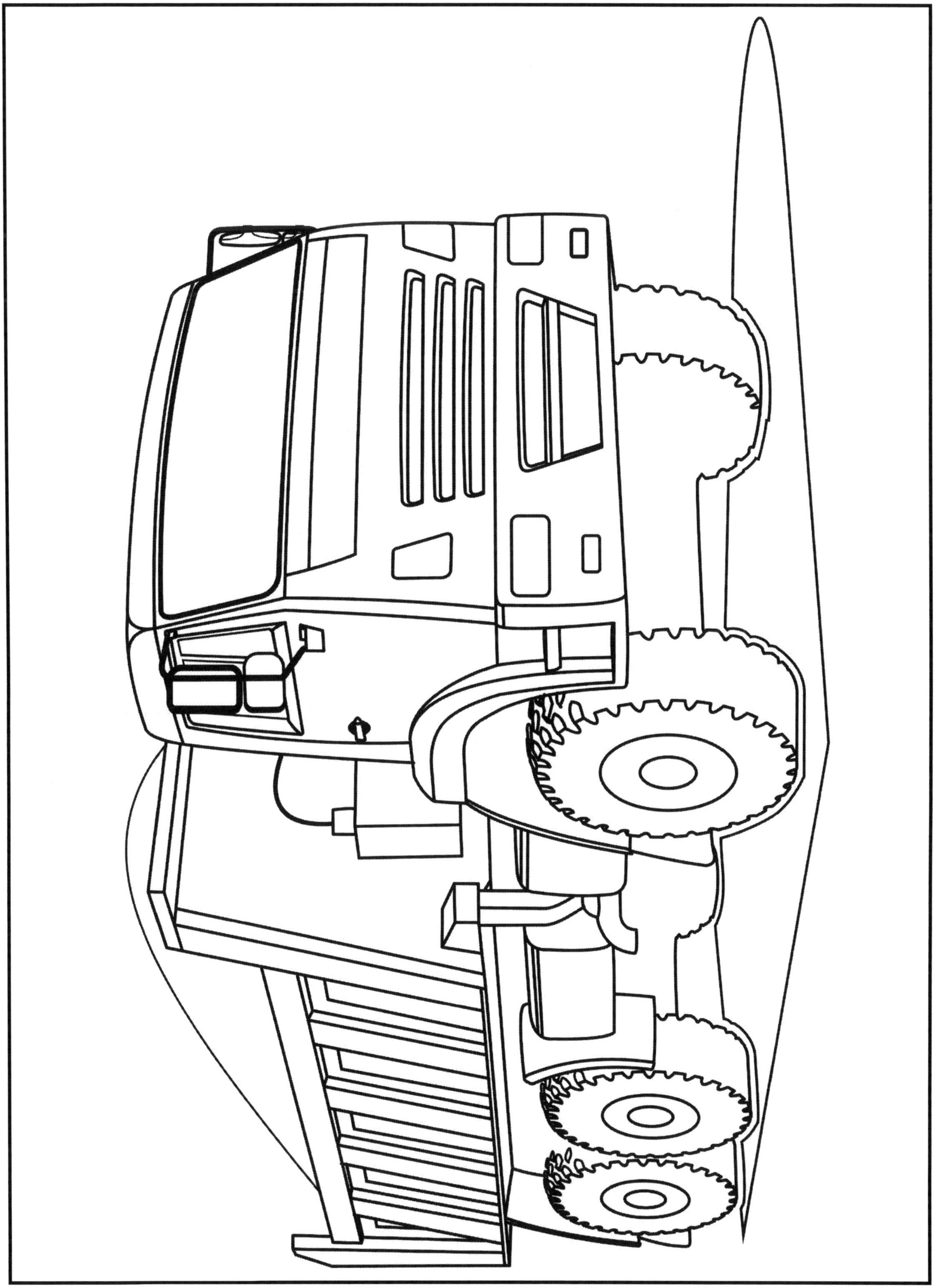

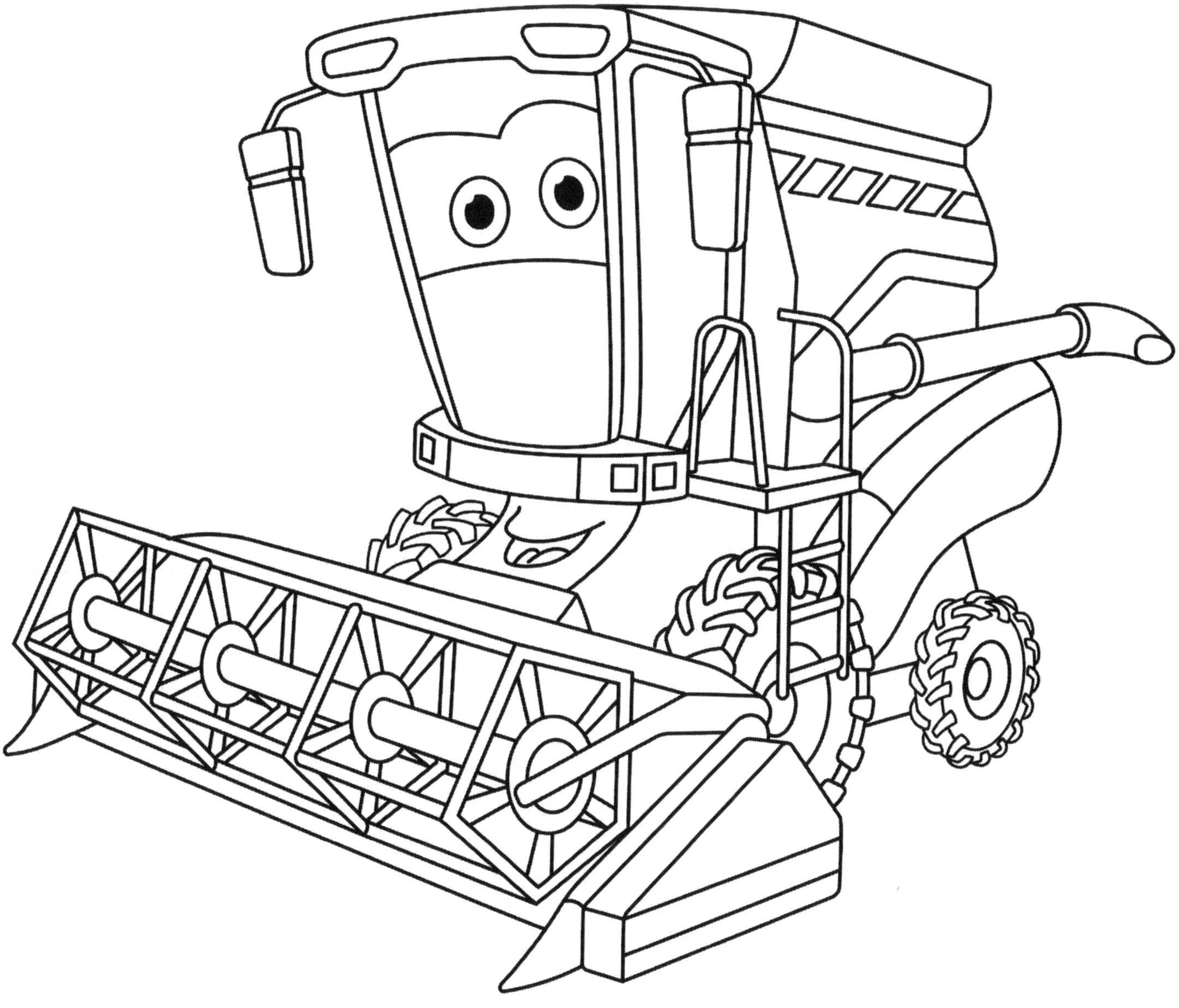

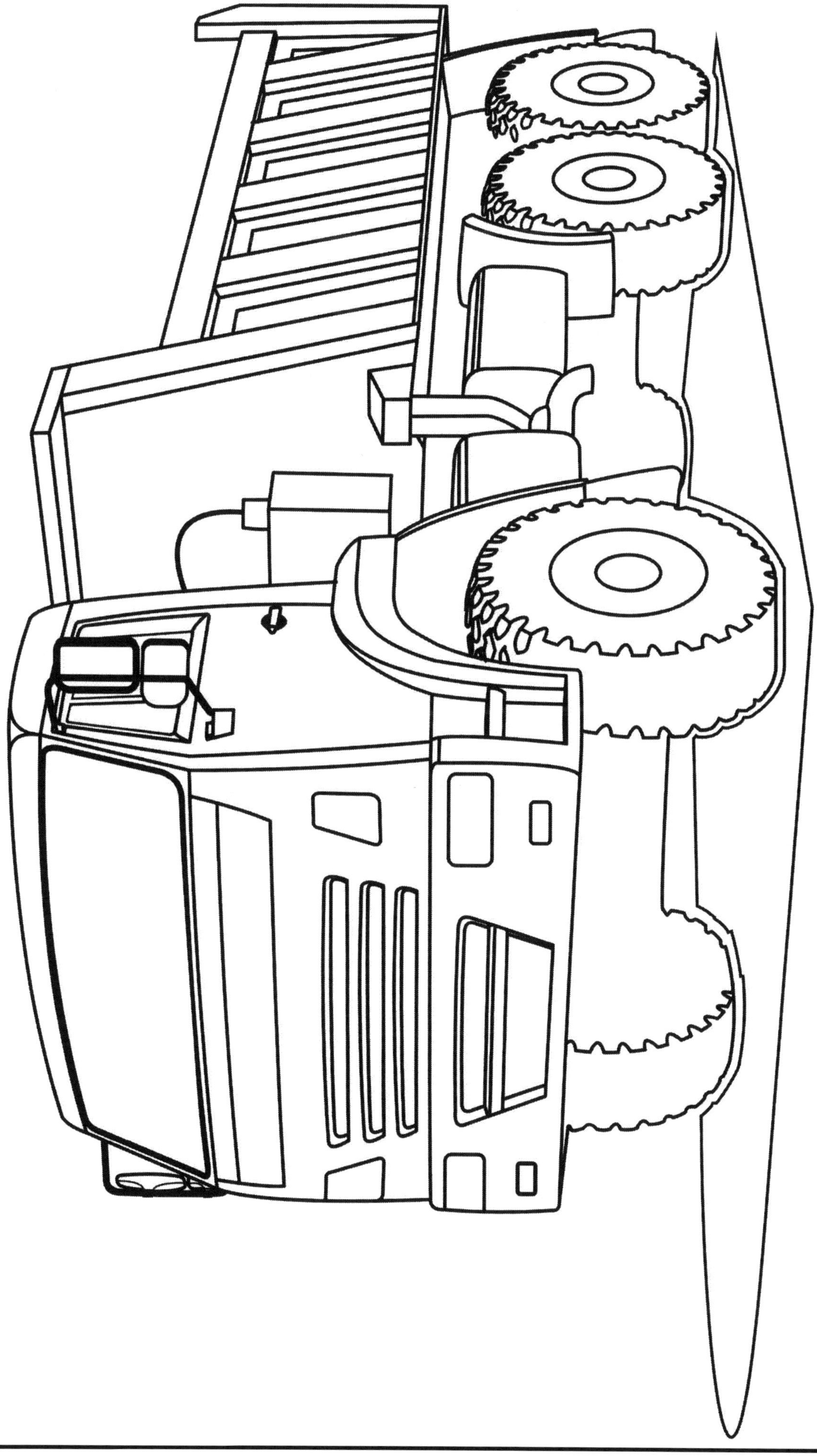

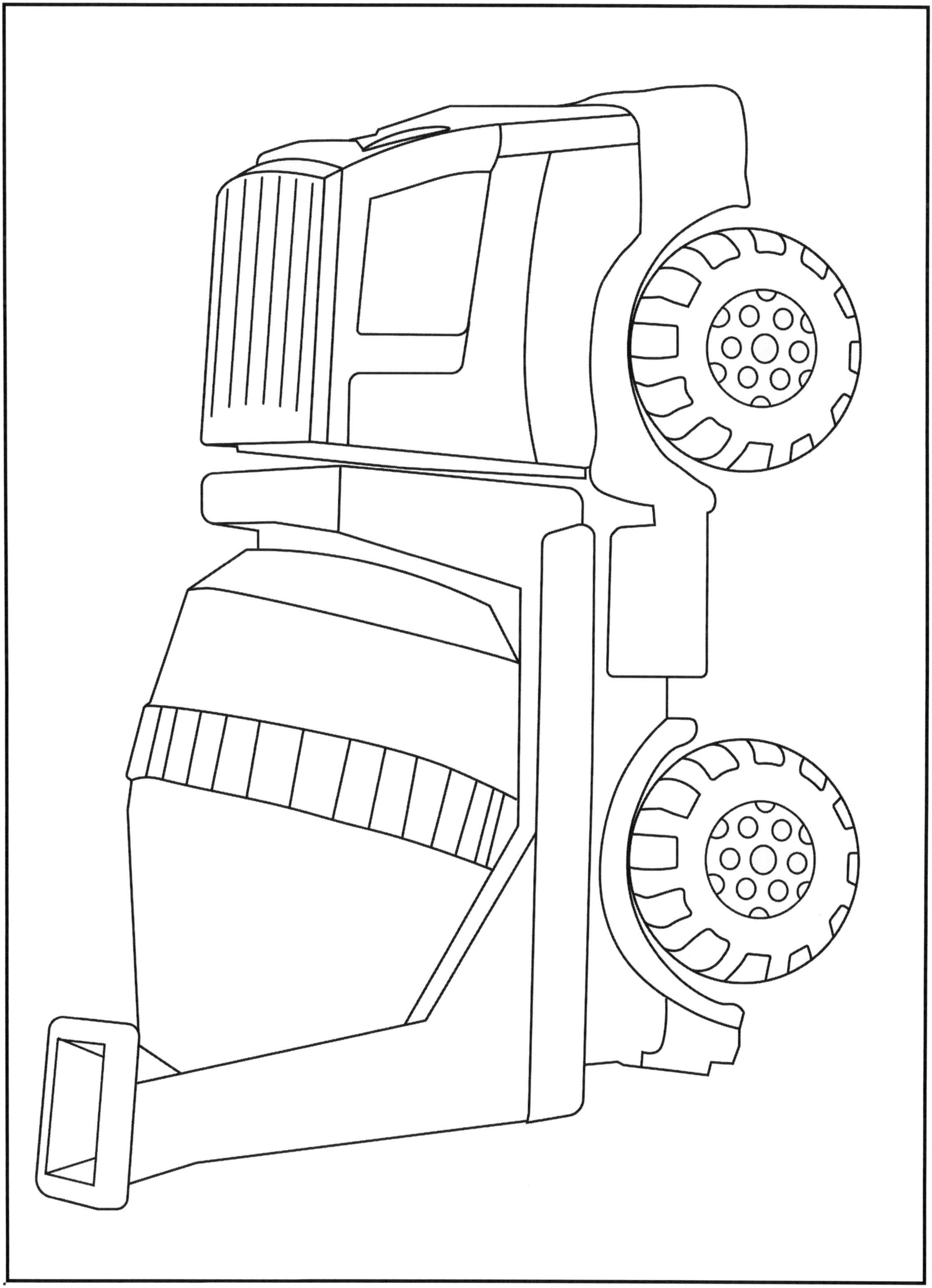

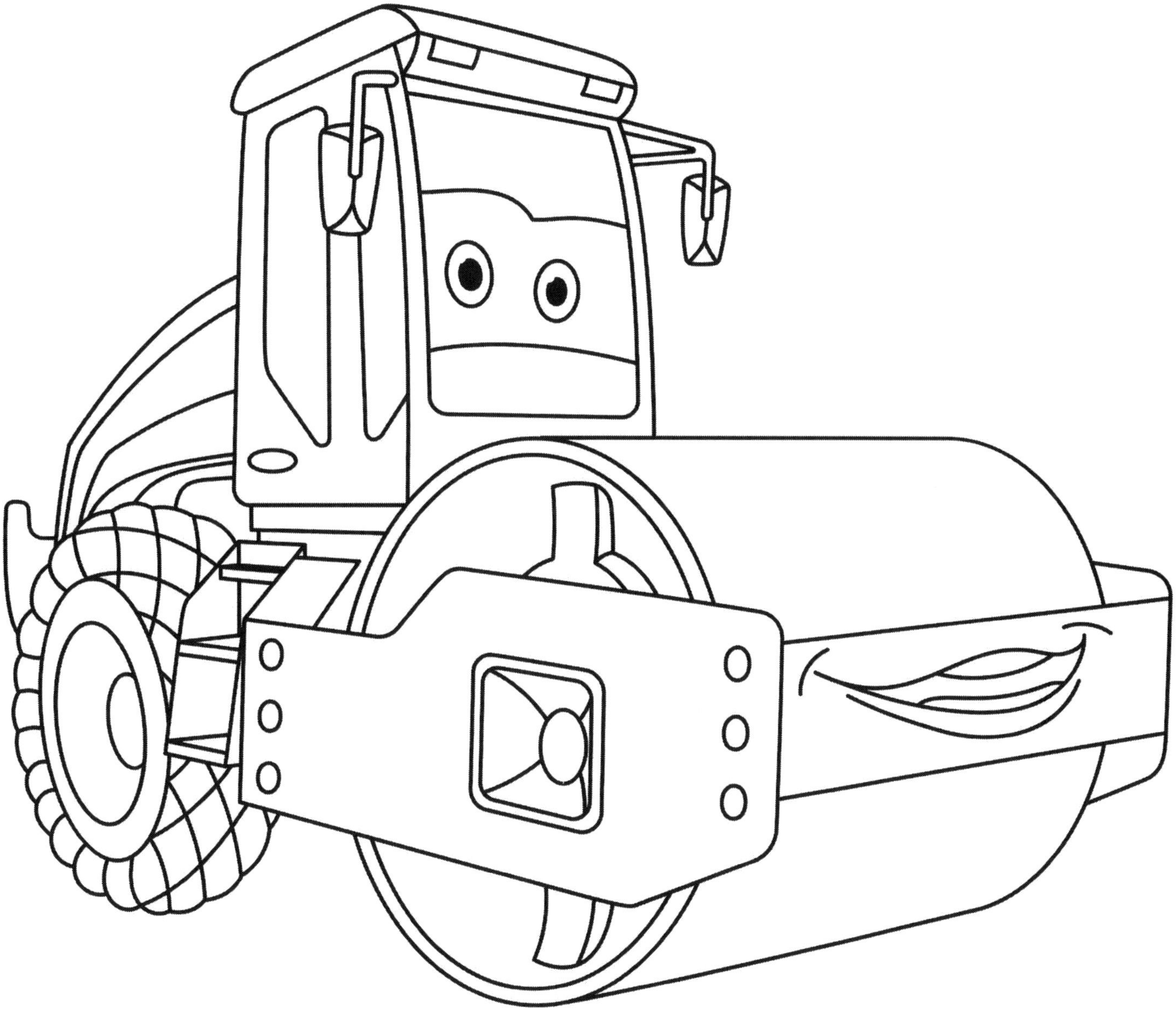

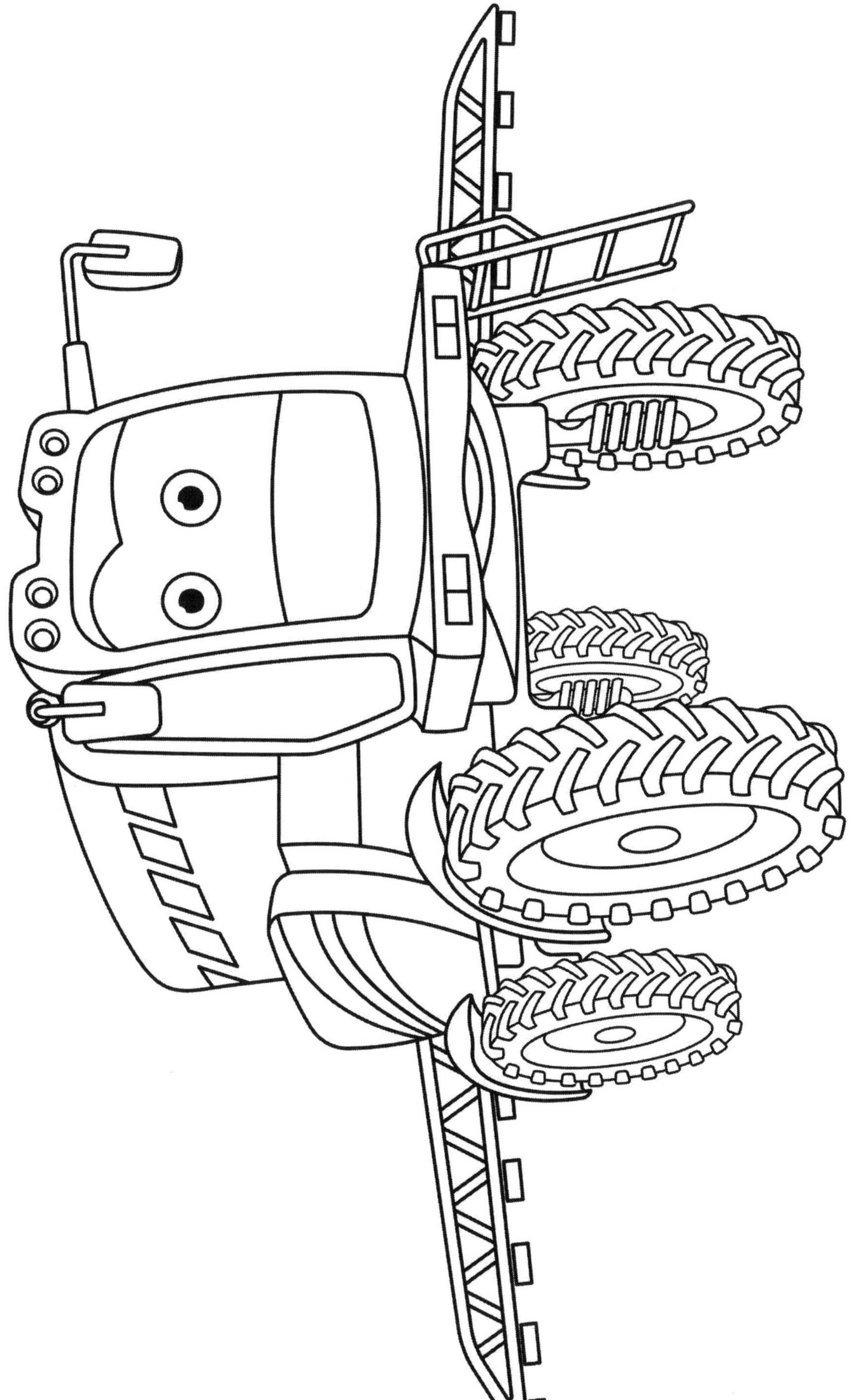

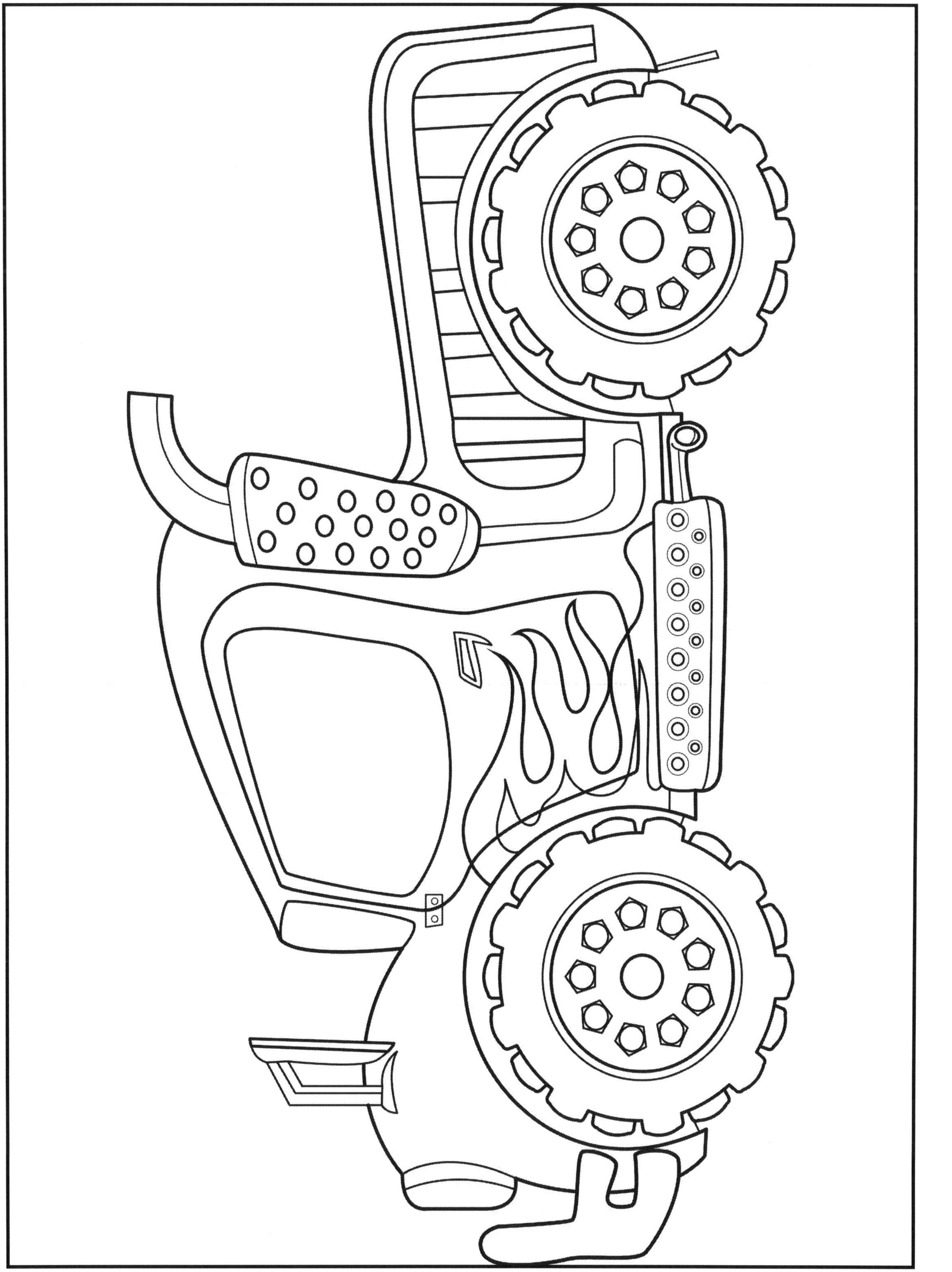

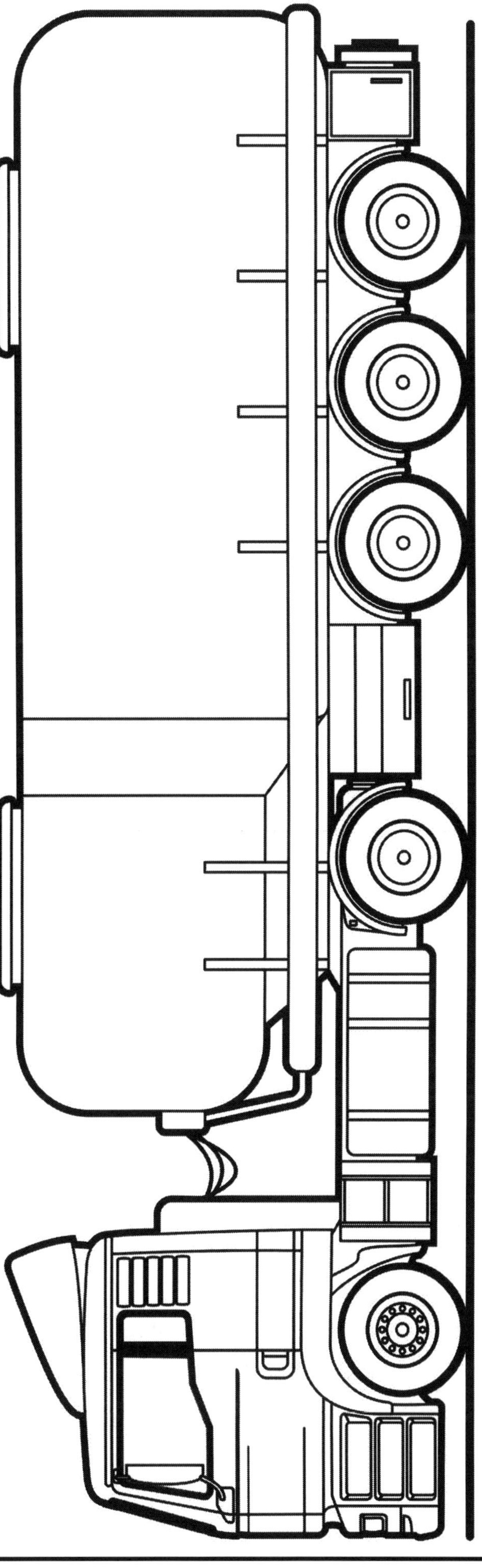

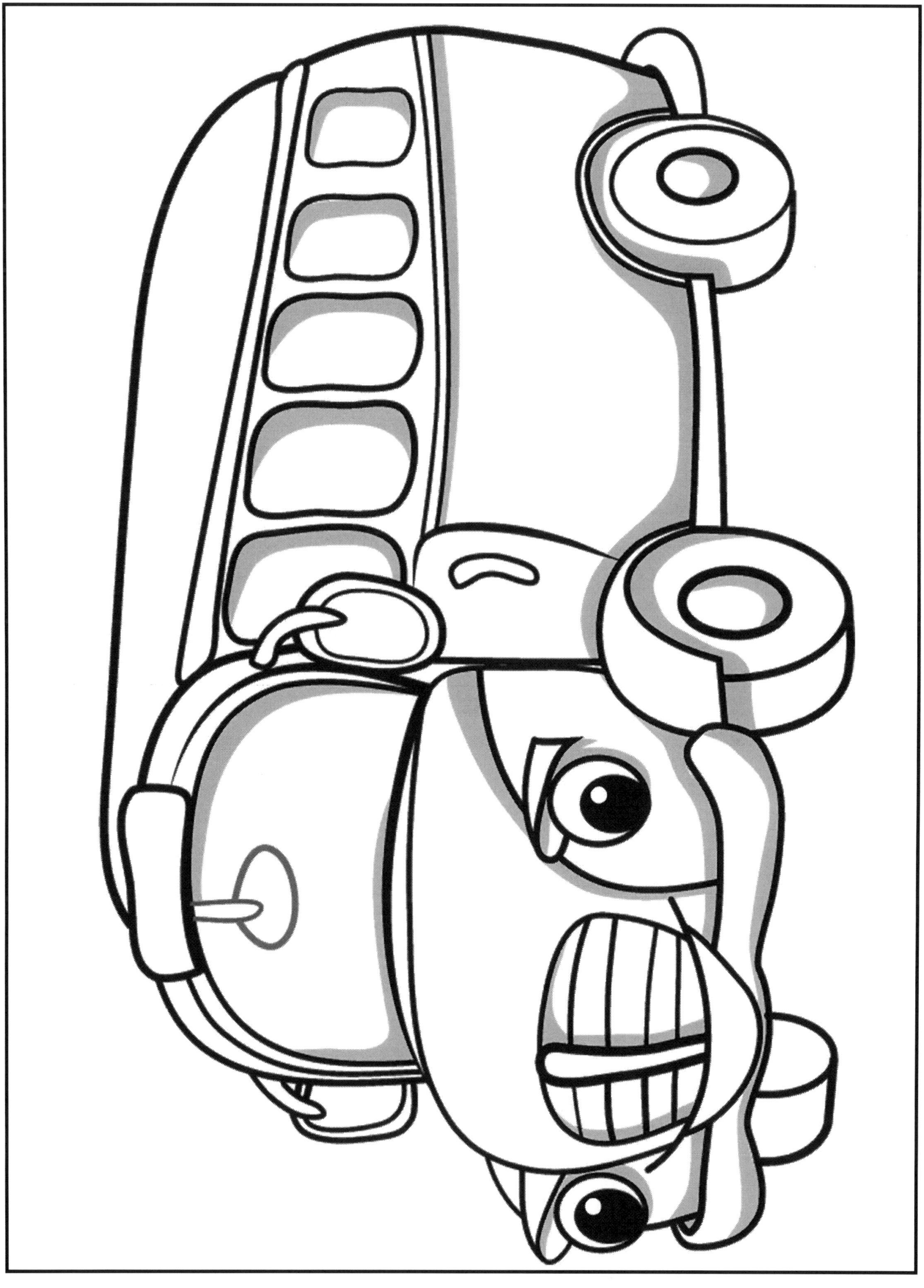

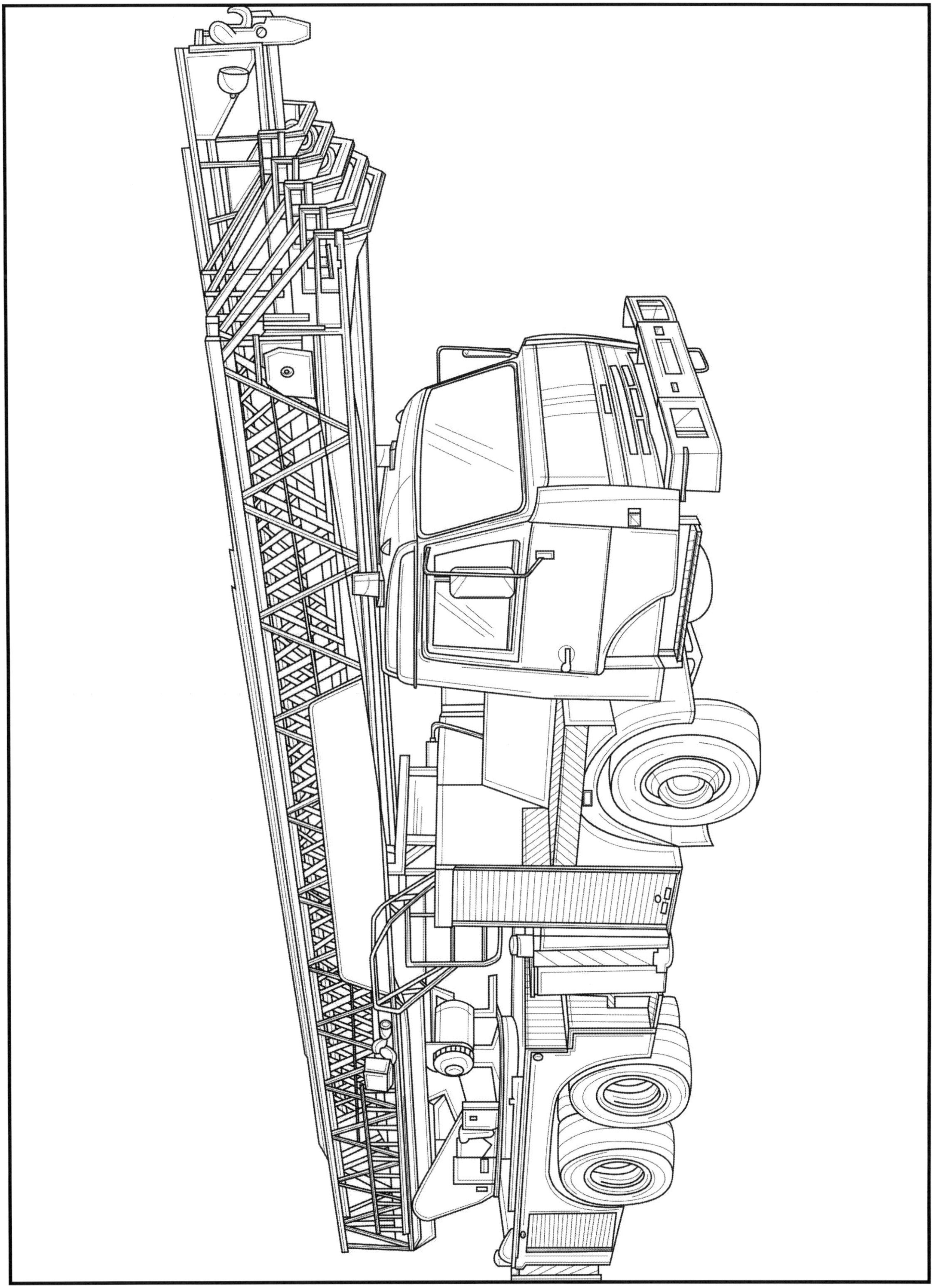

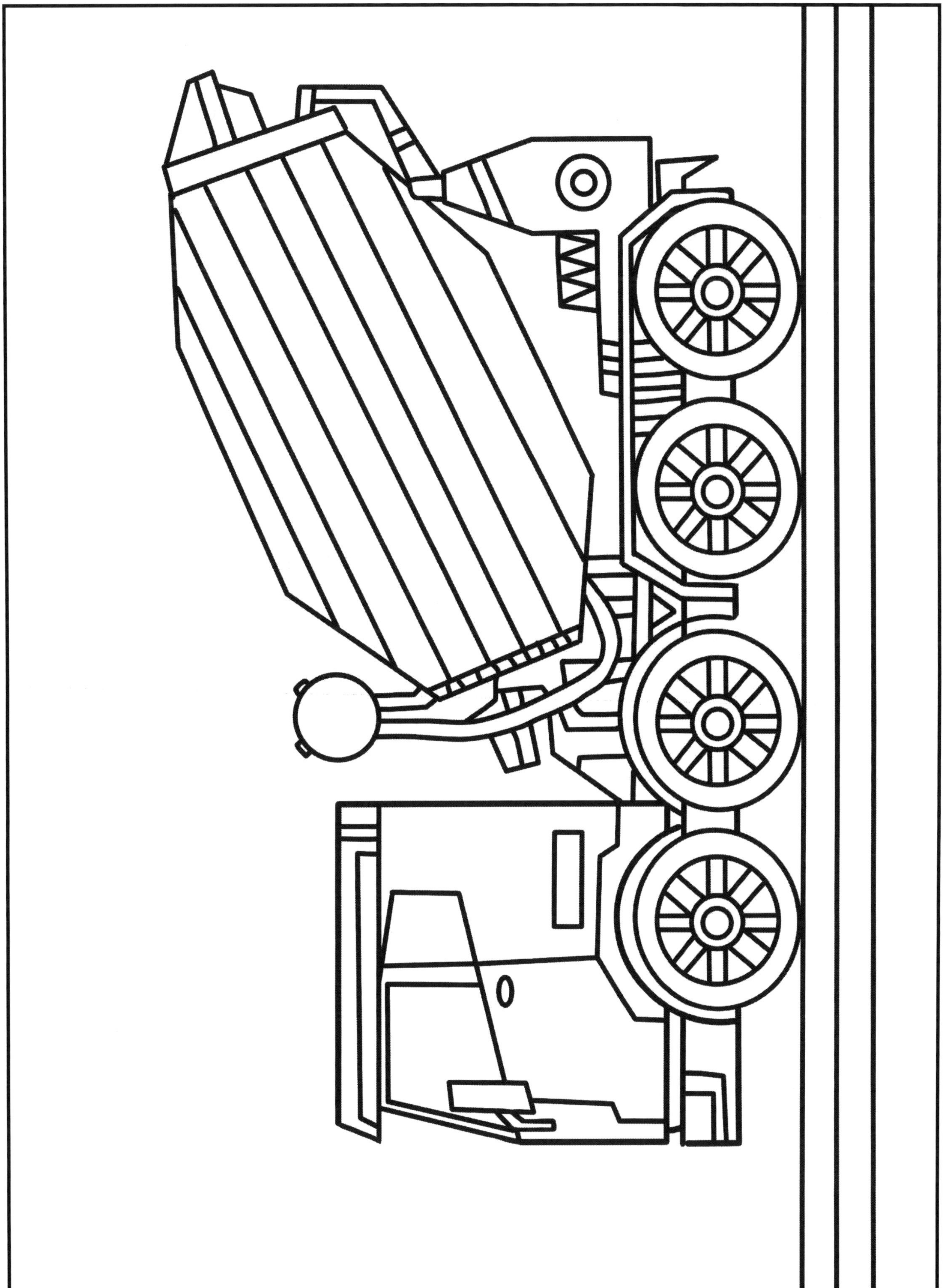

GARAGE

tribo

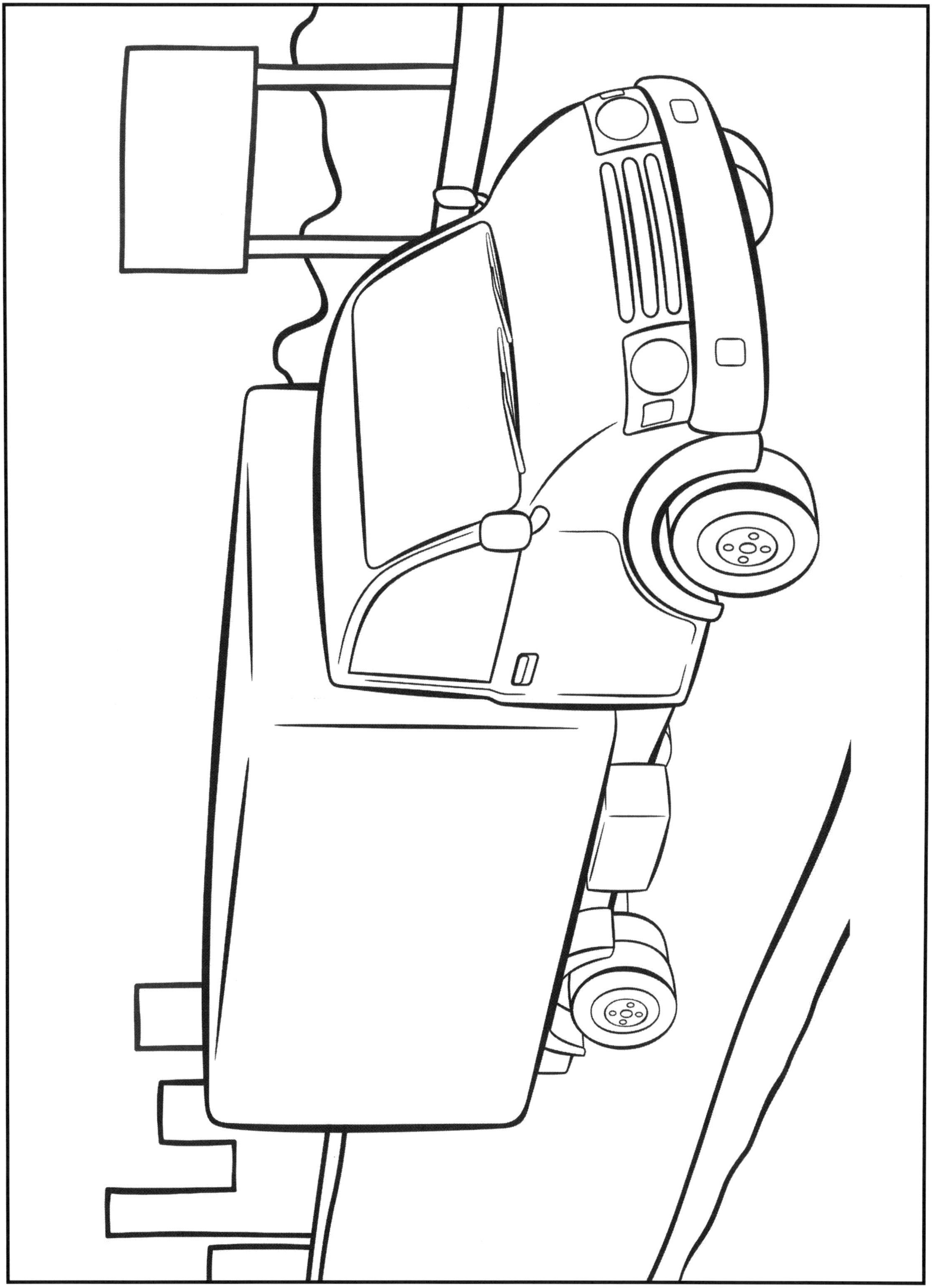

D.U.M.P
TRUCK
315

EMERGENCY
AMBULANCE

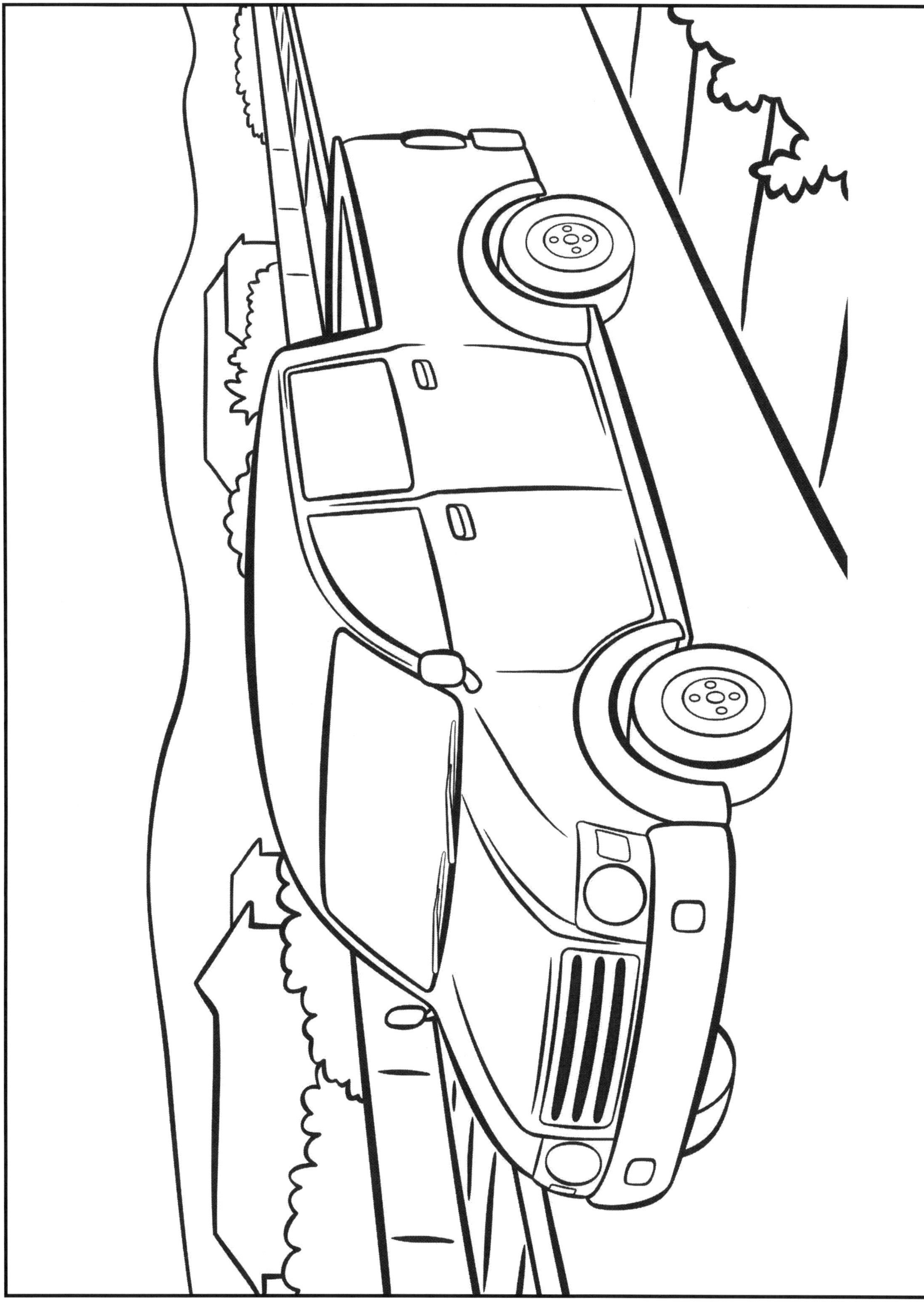

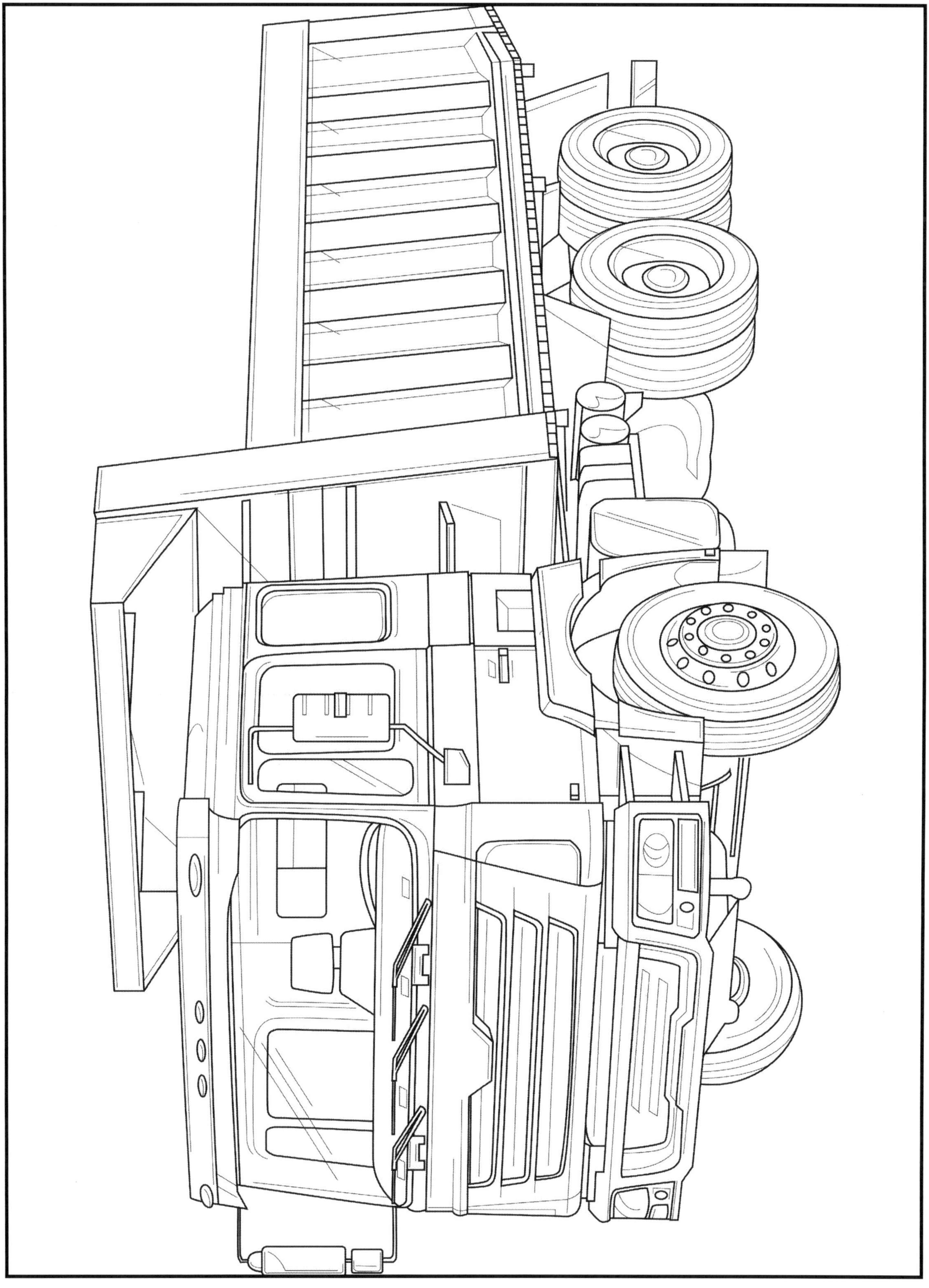

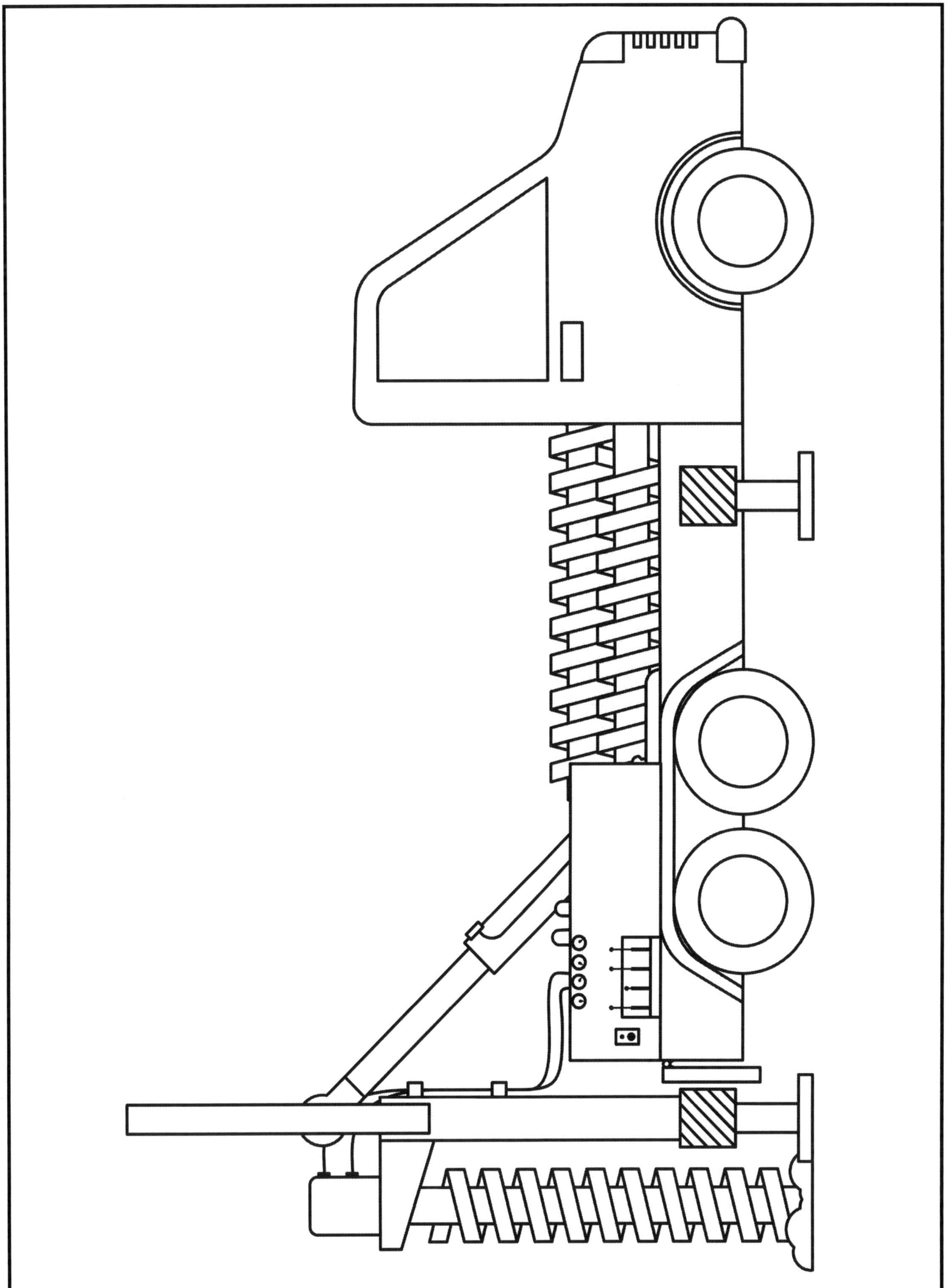

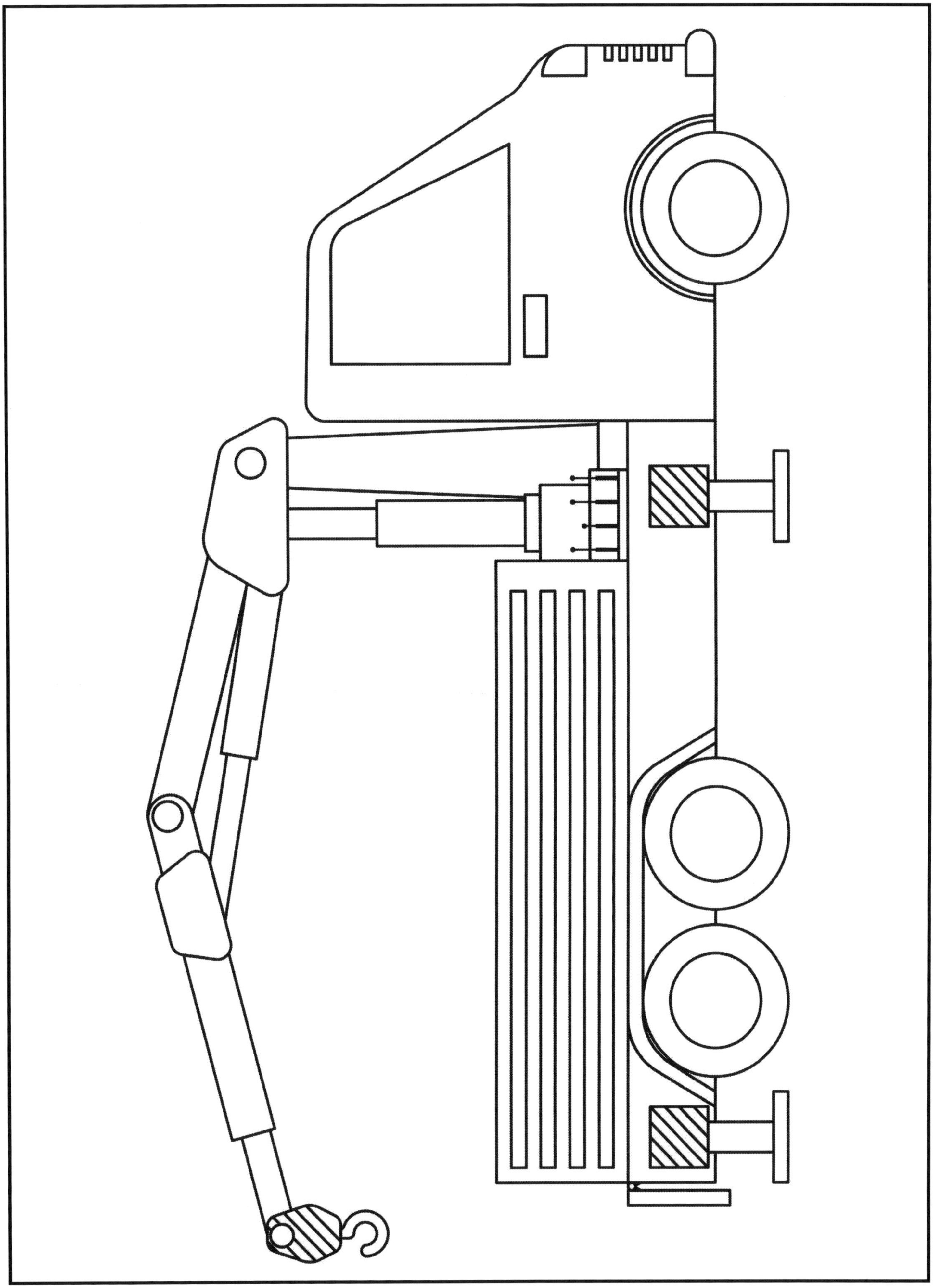

MONSTER
TRUCKS

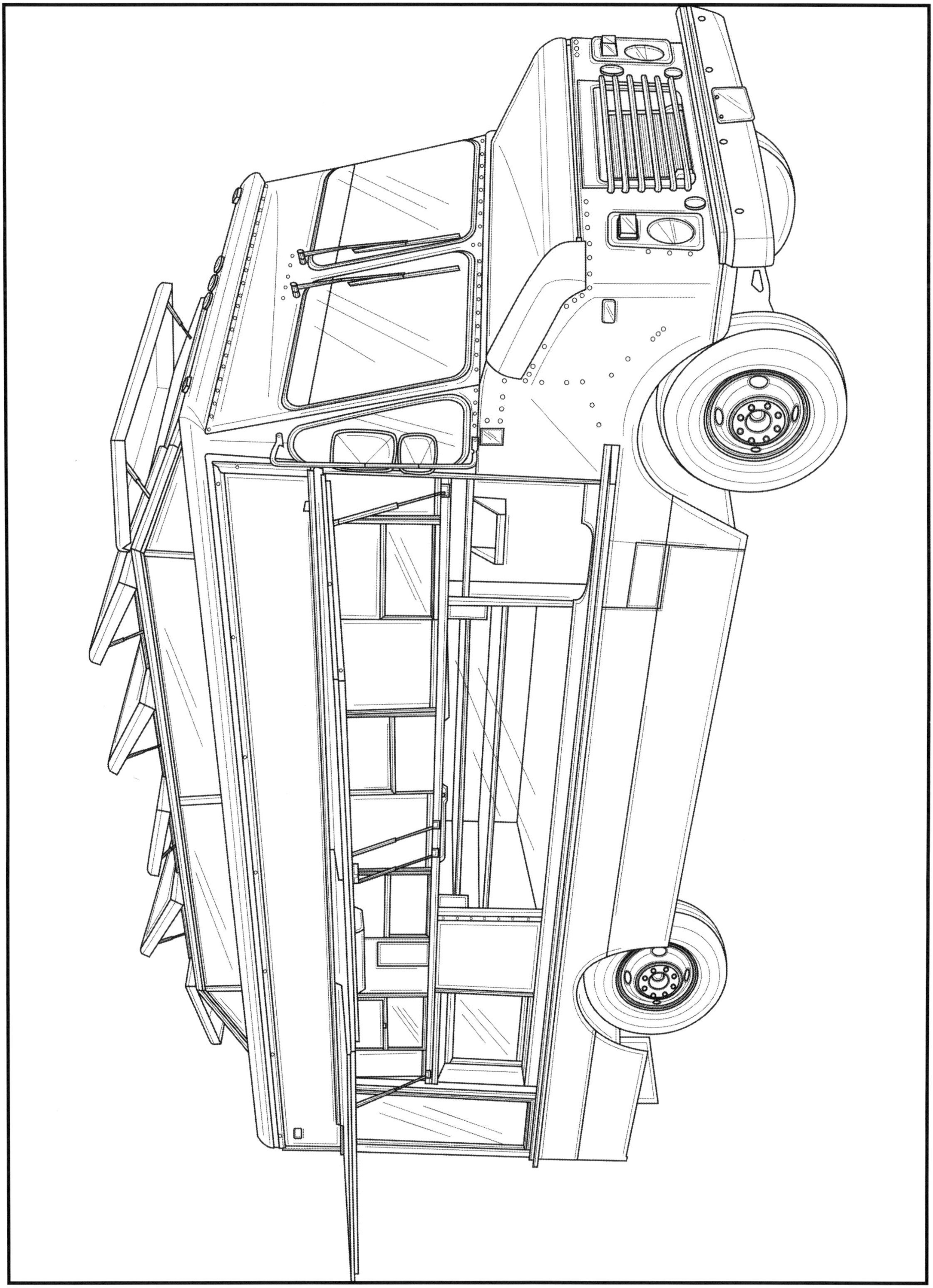

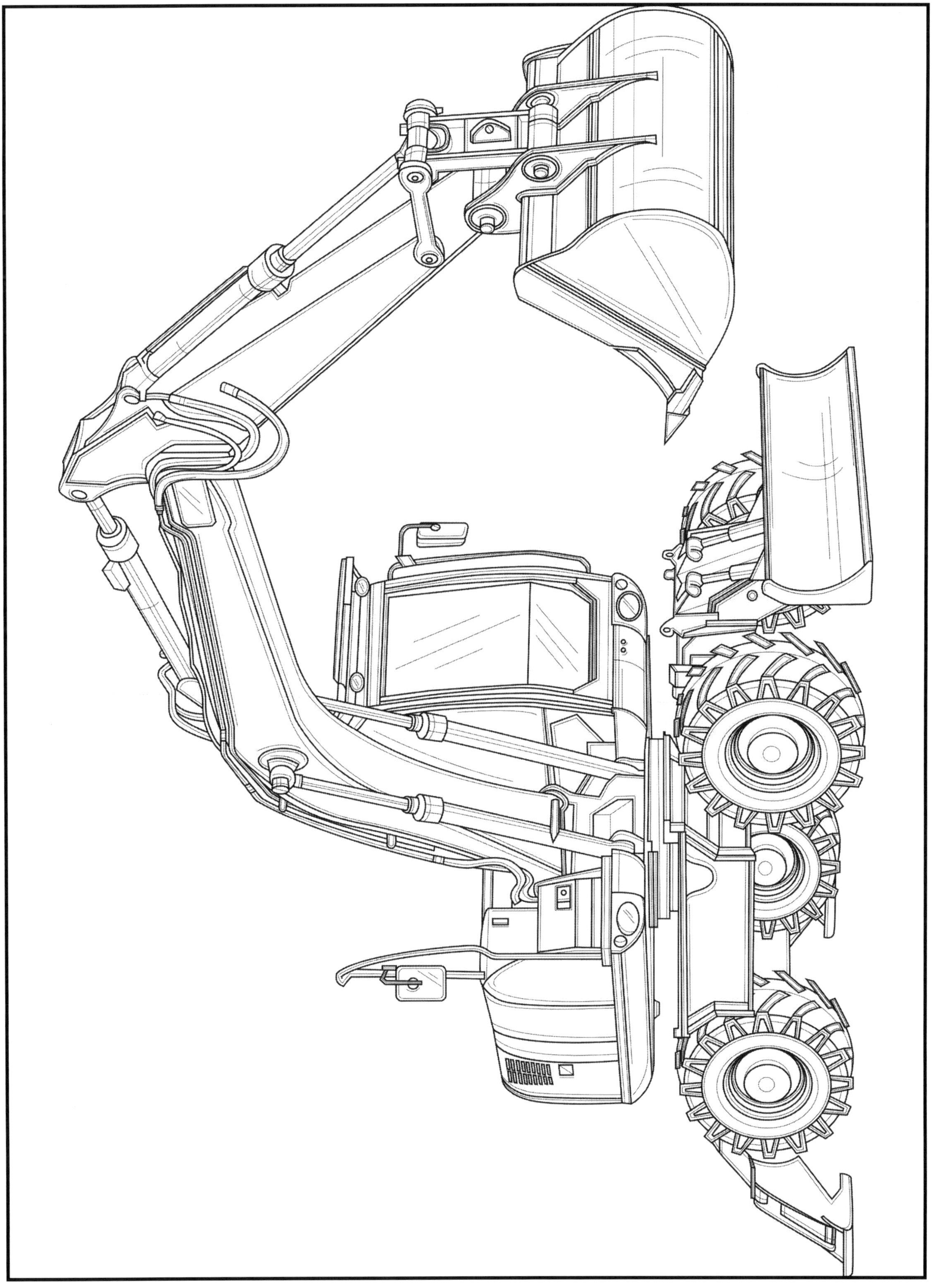

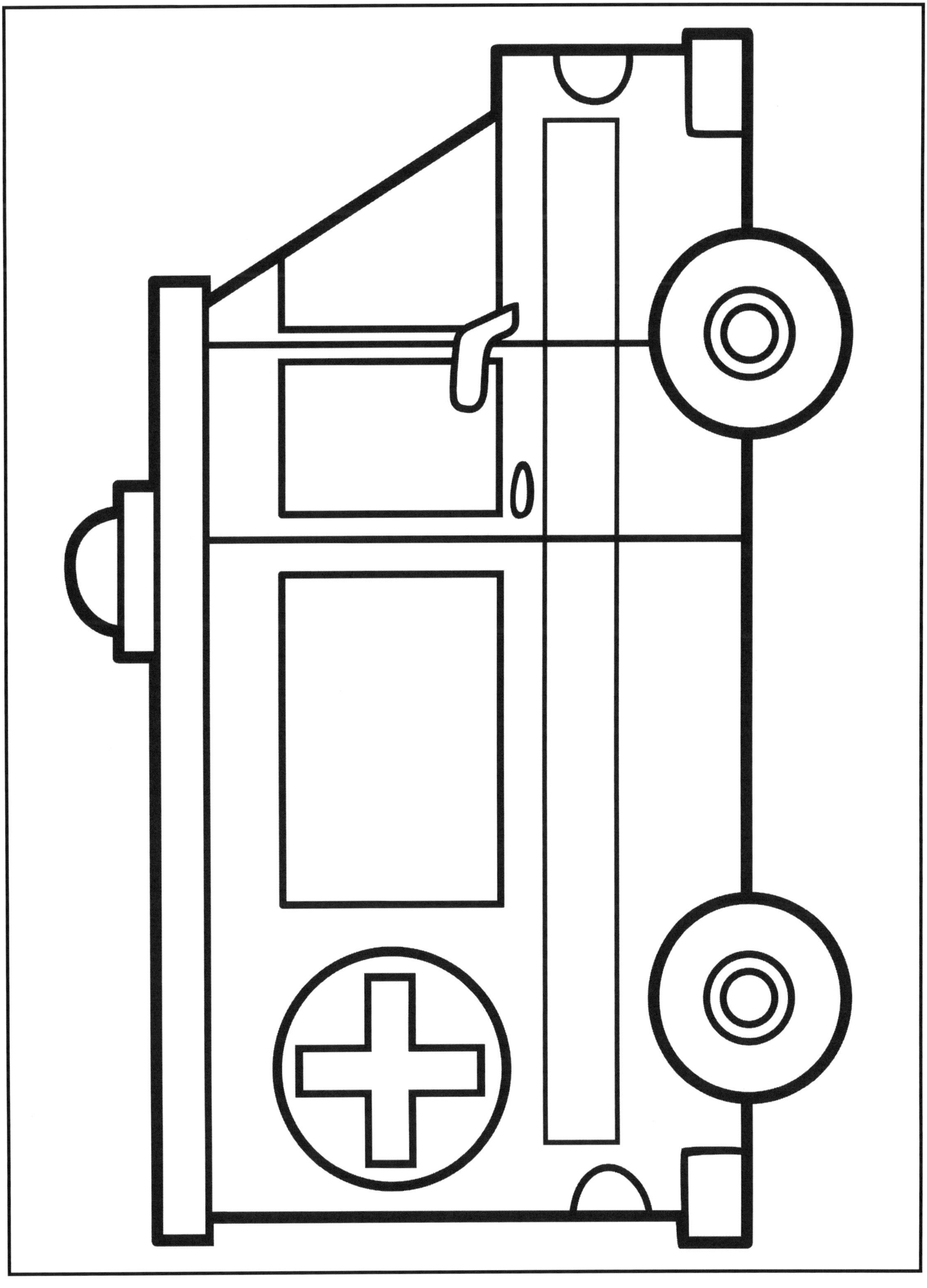

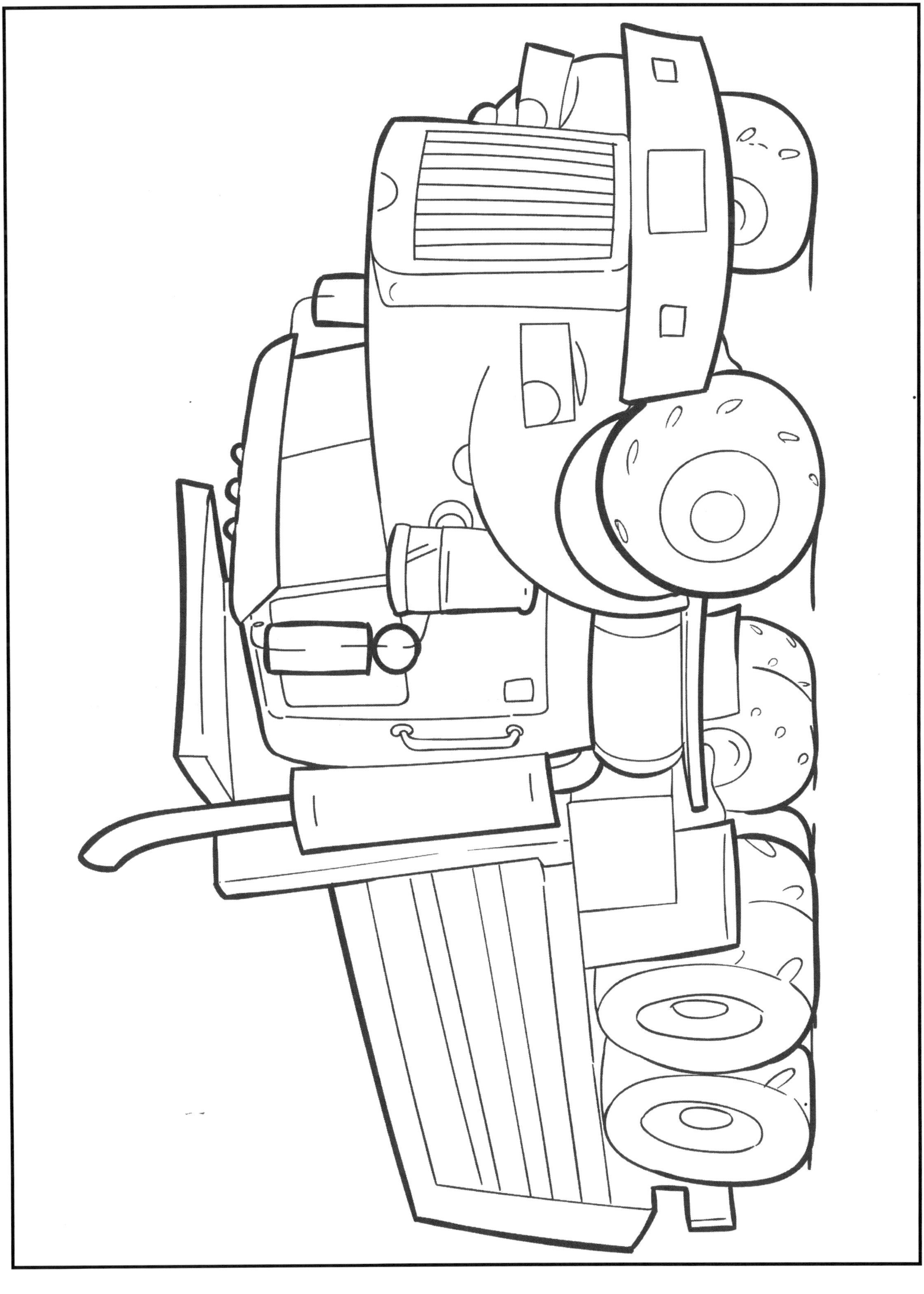

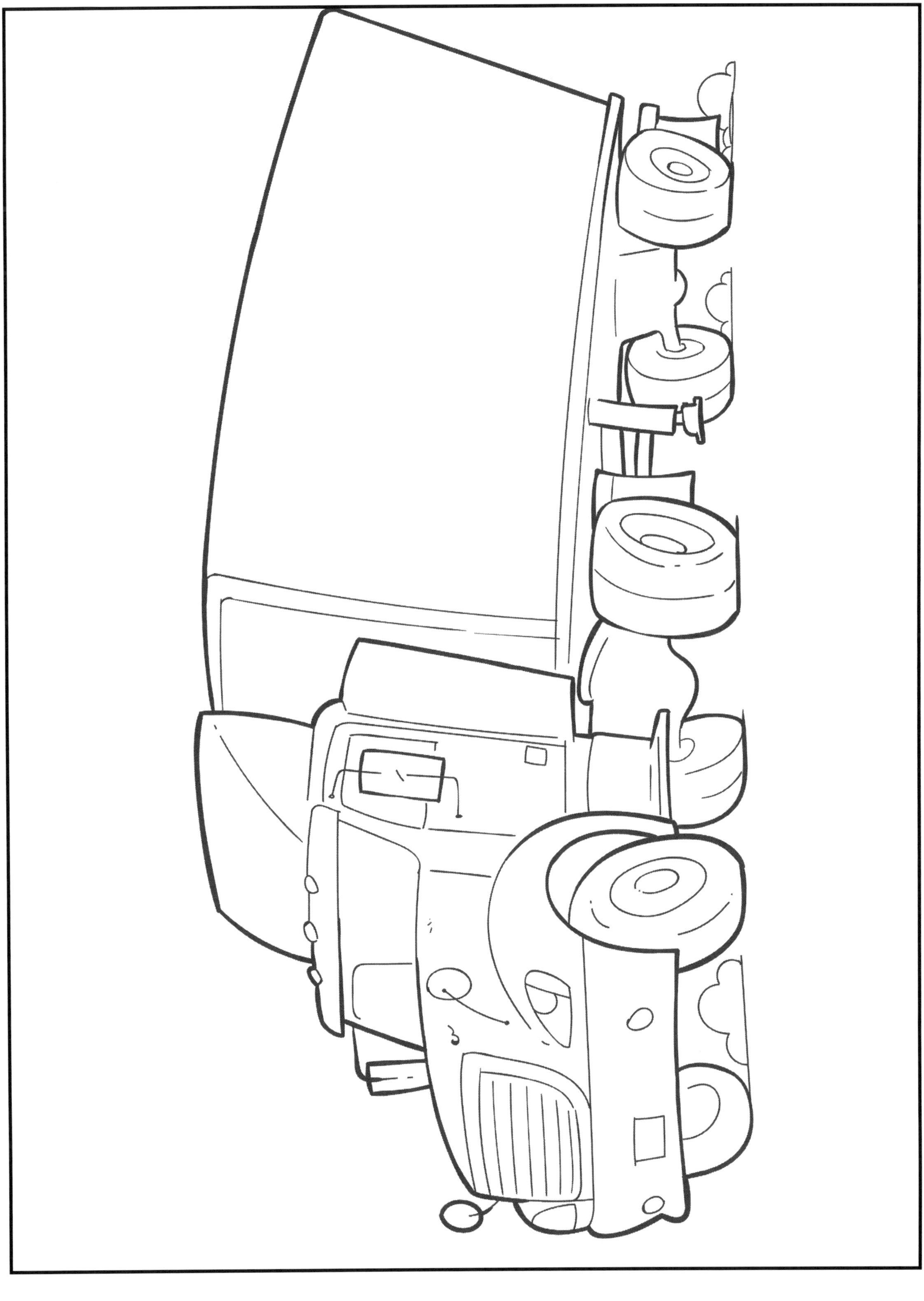

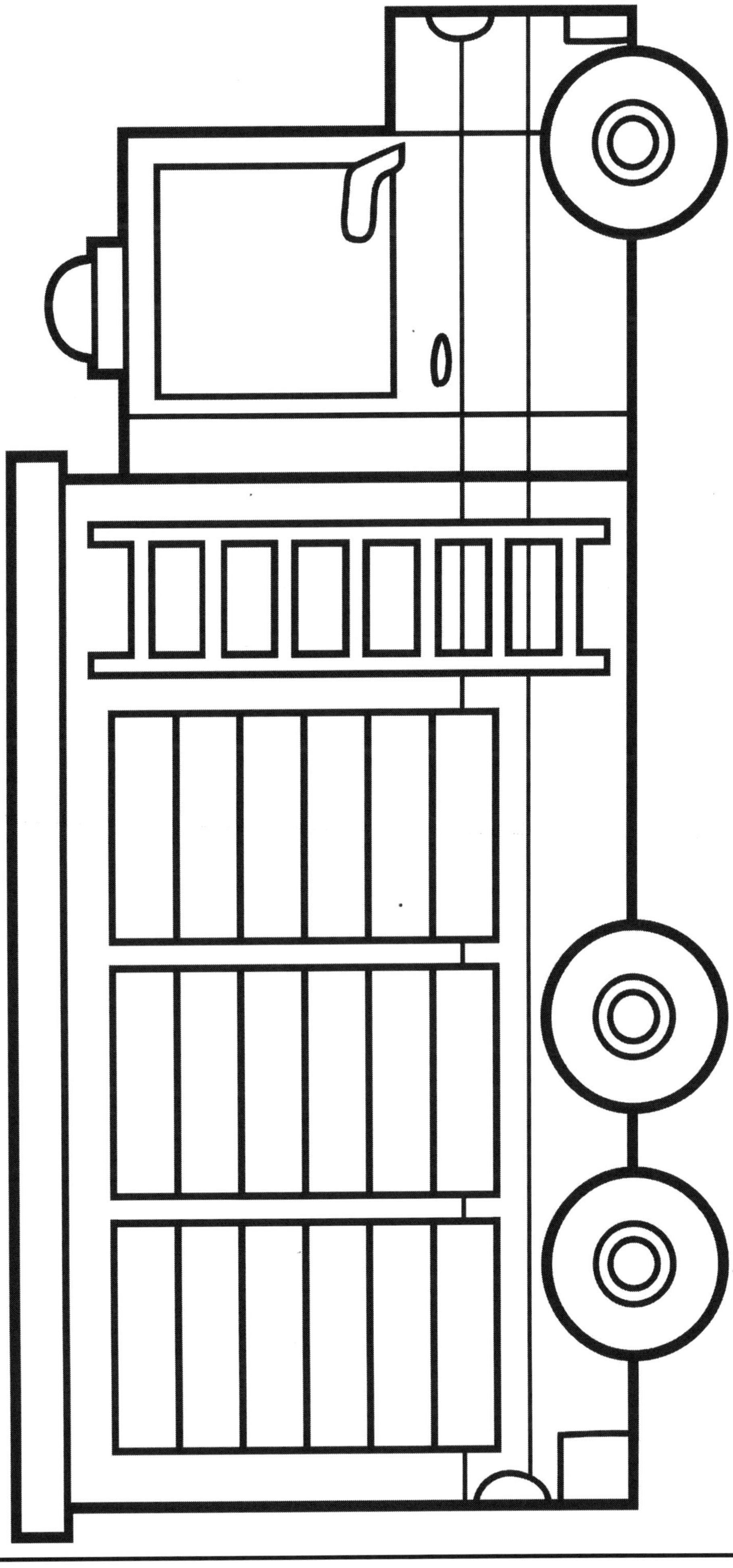

AMBULANCE

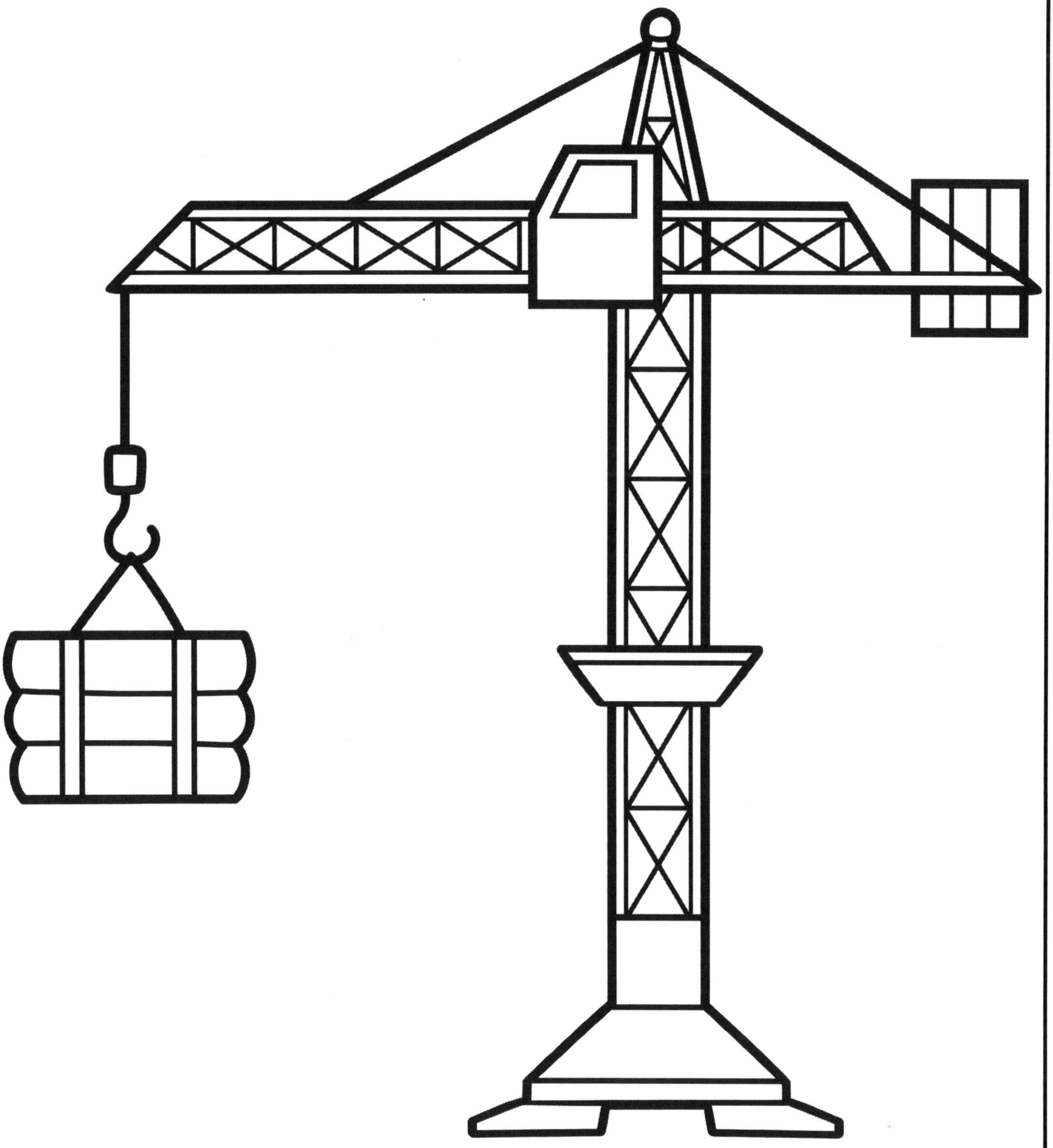

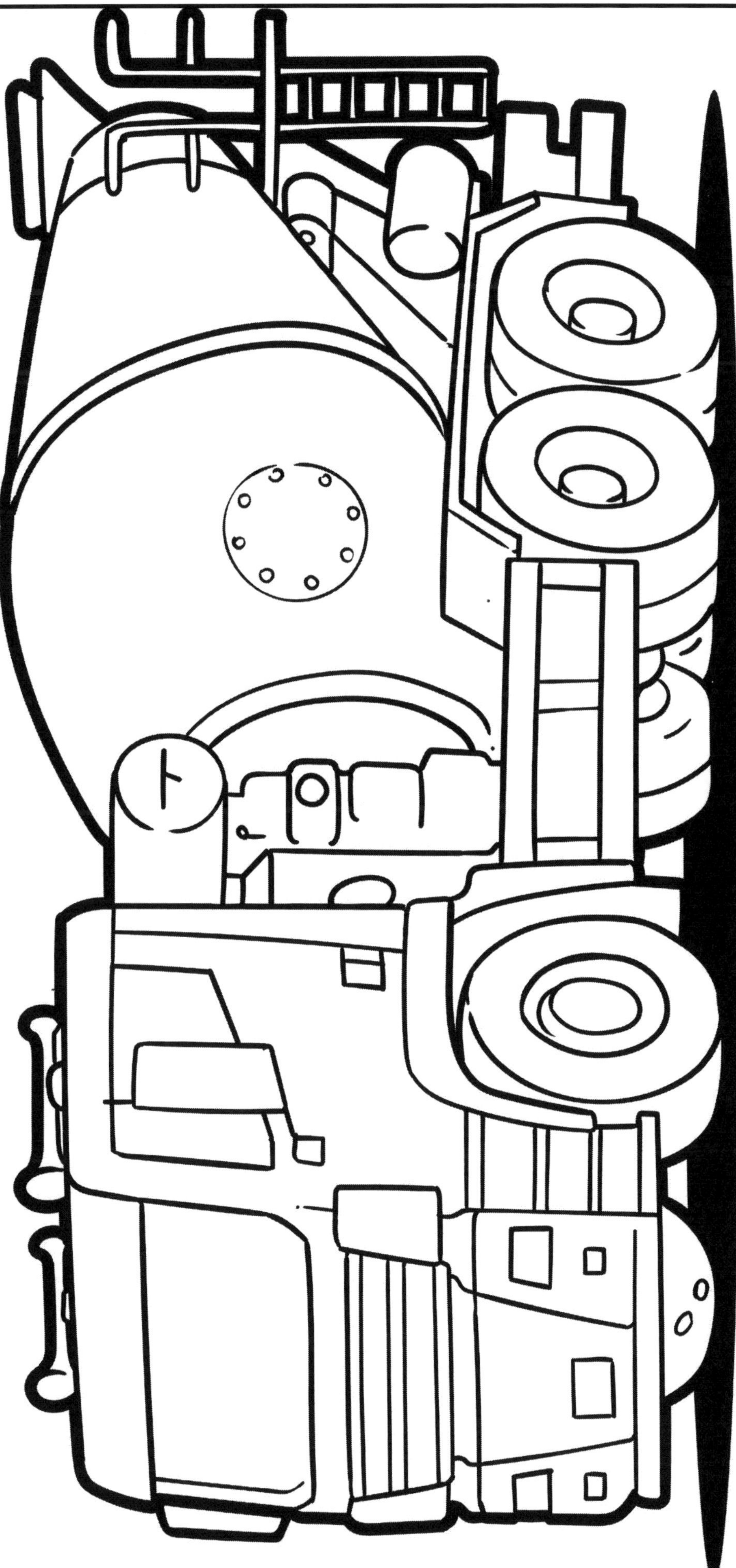

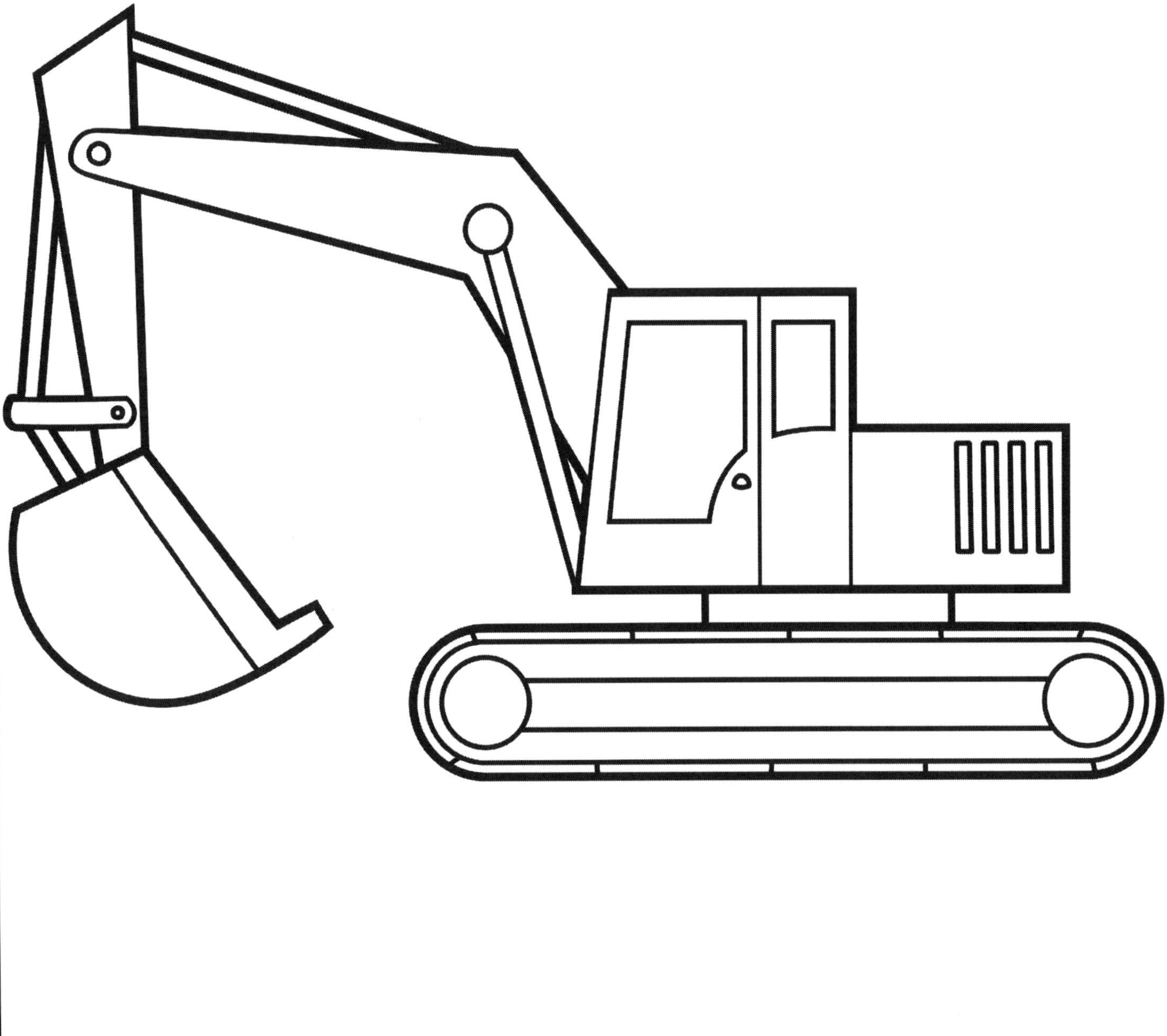

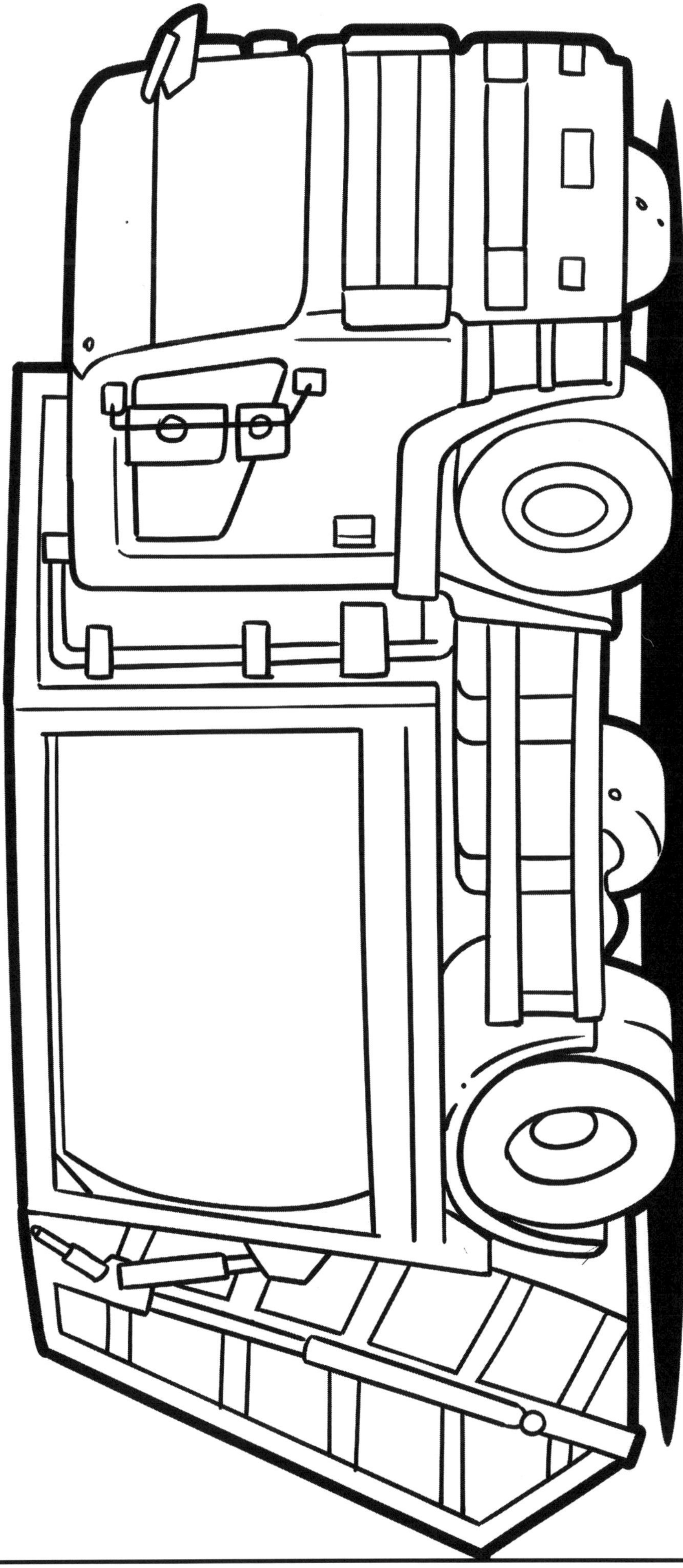

COAL

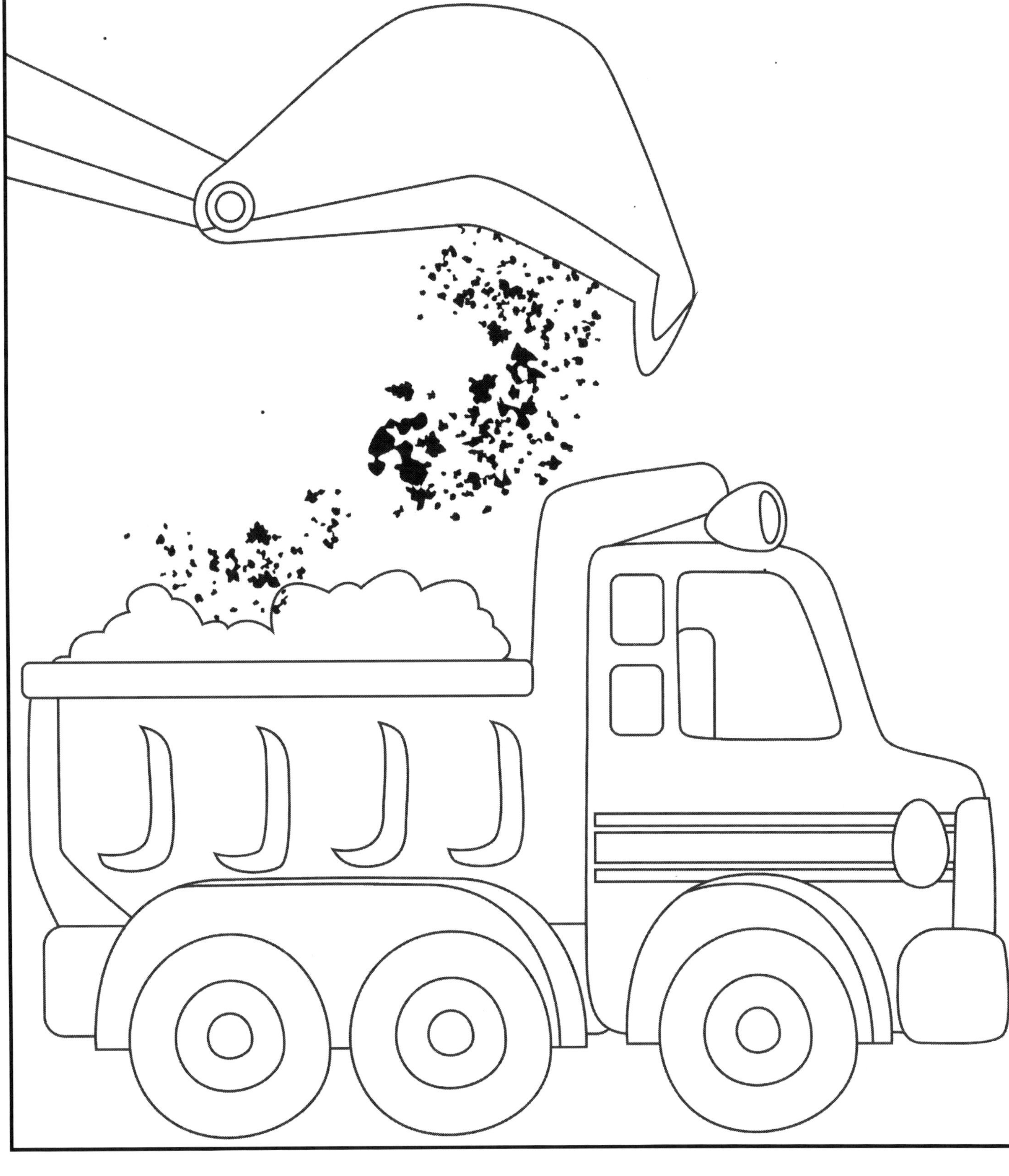

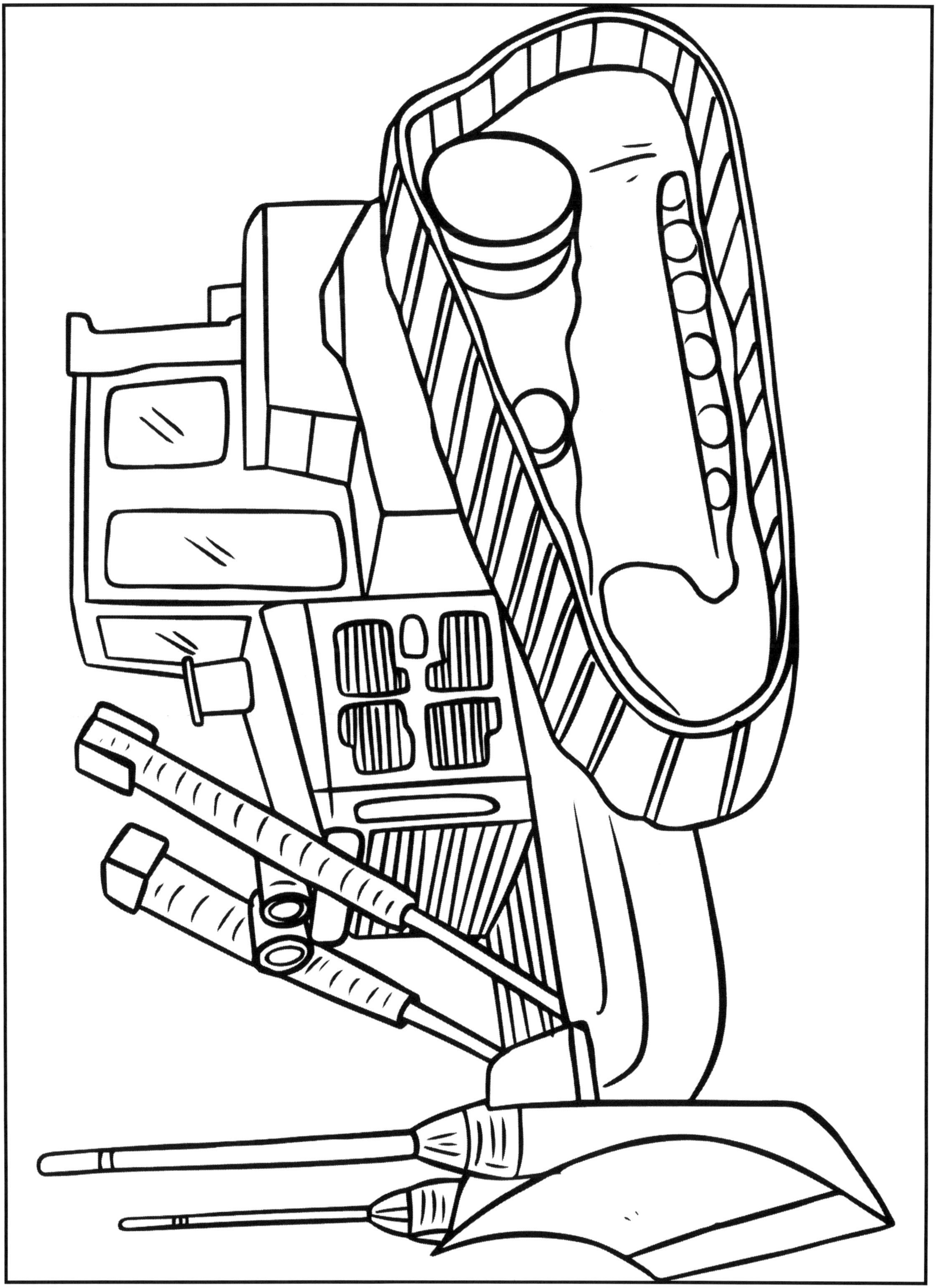

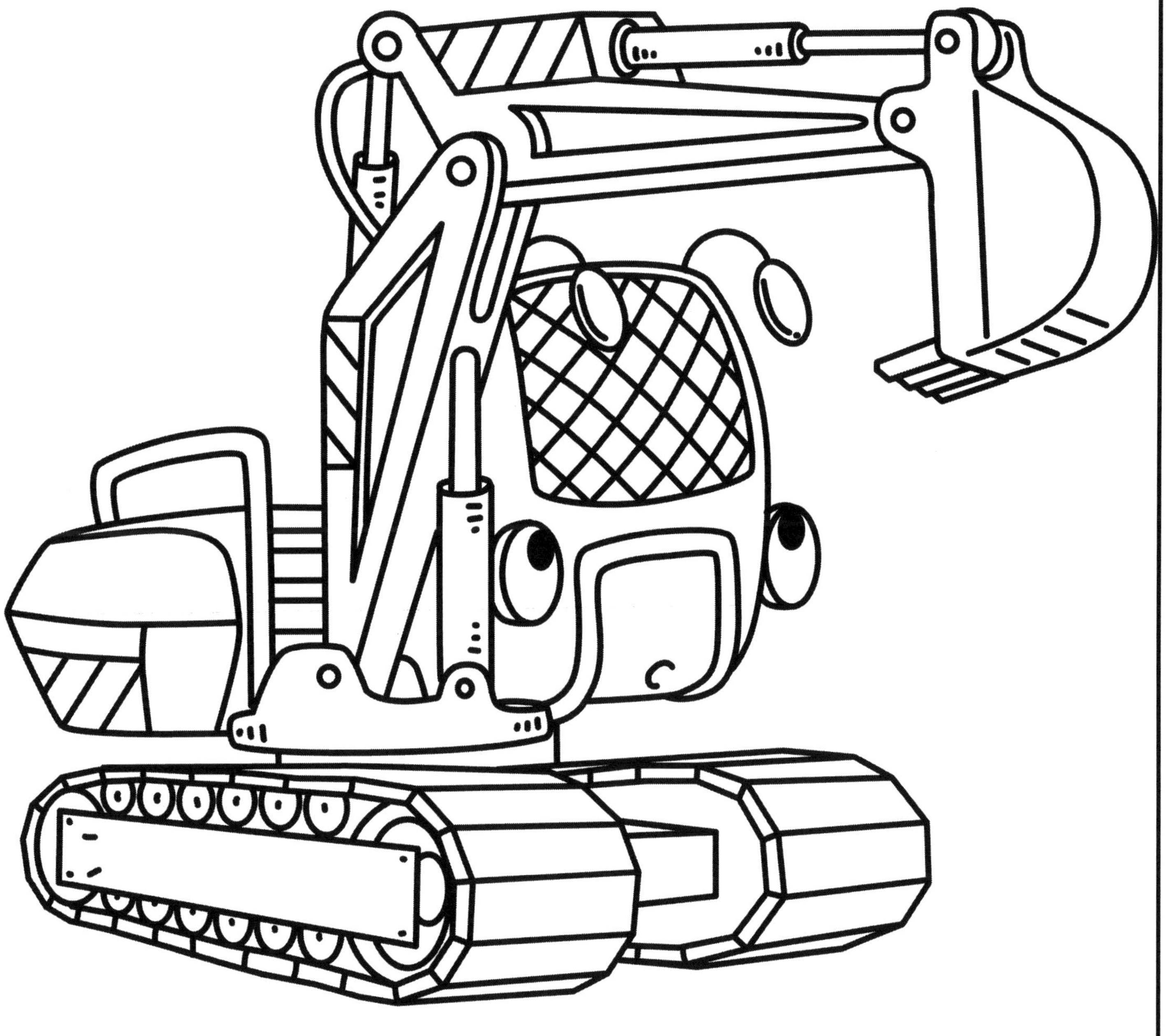

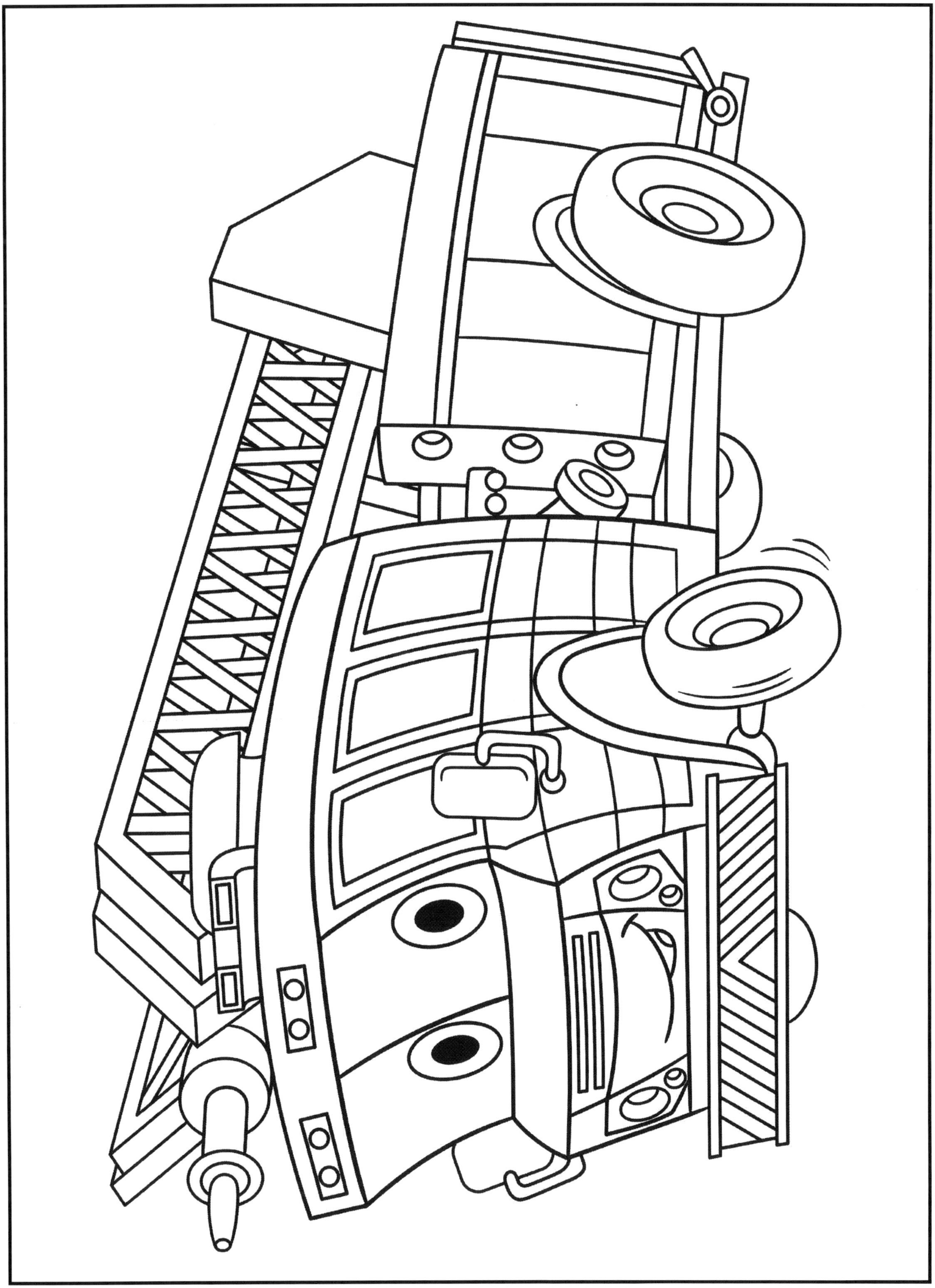

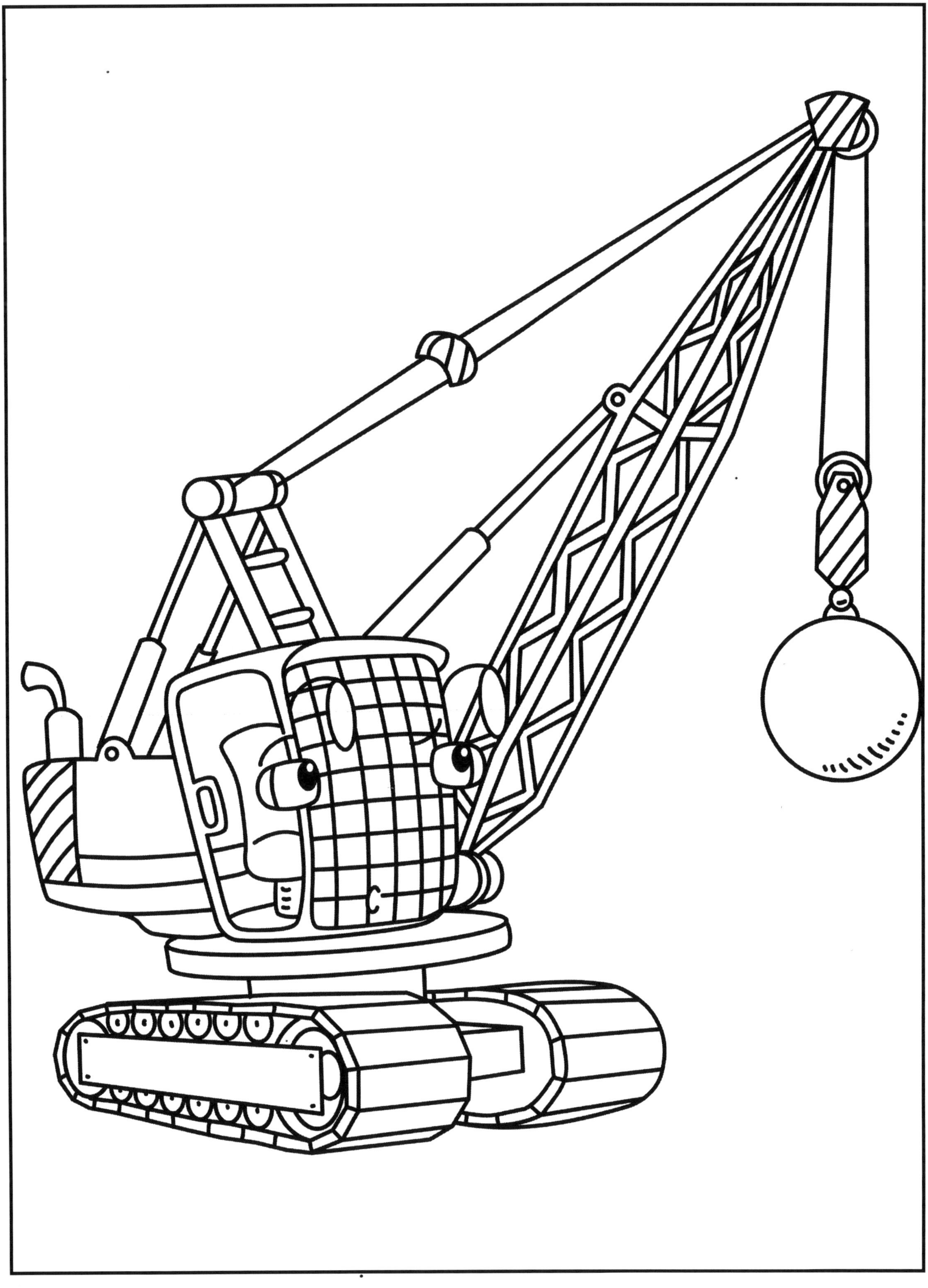
C

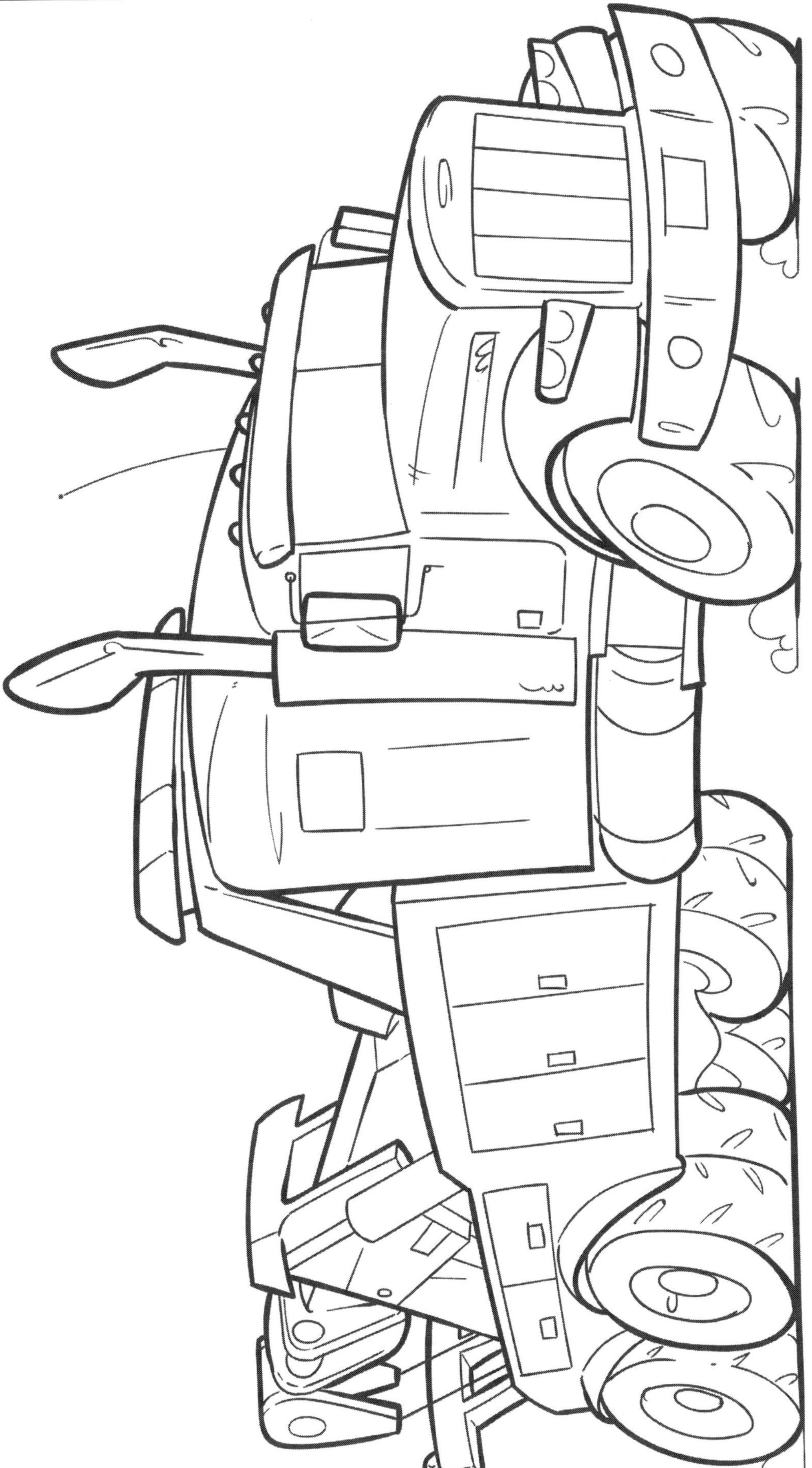

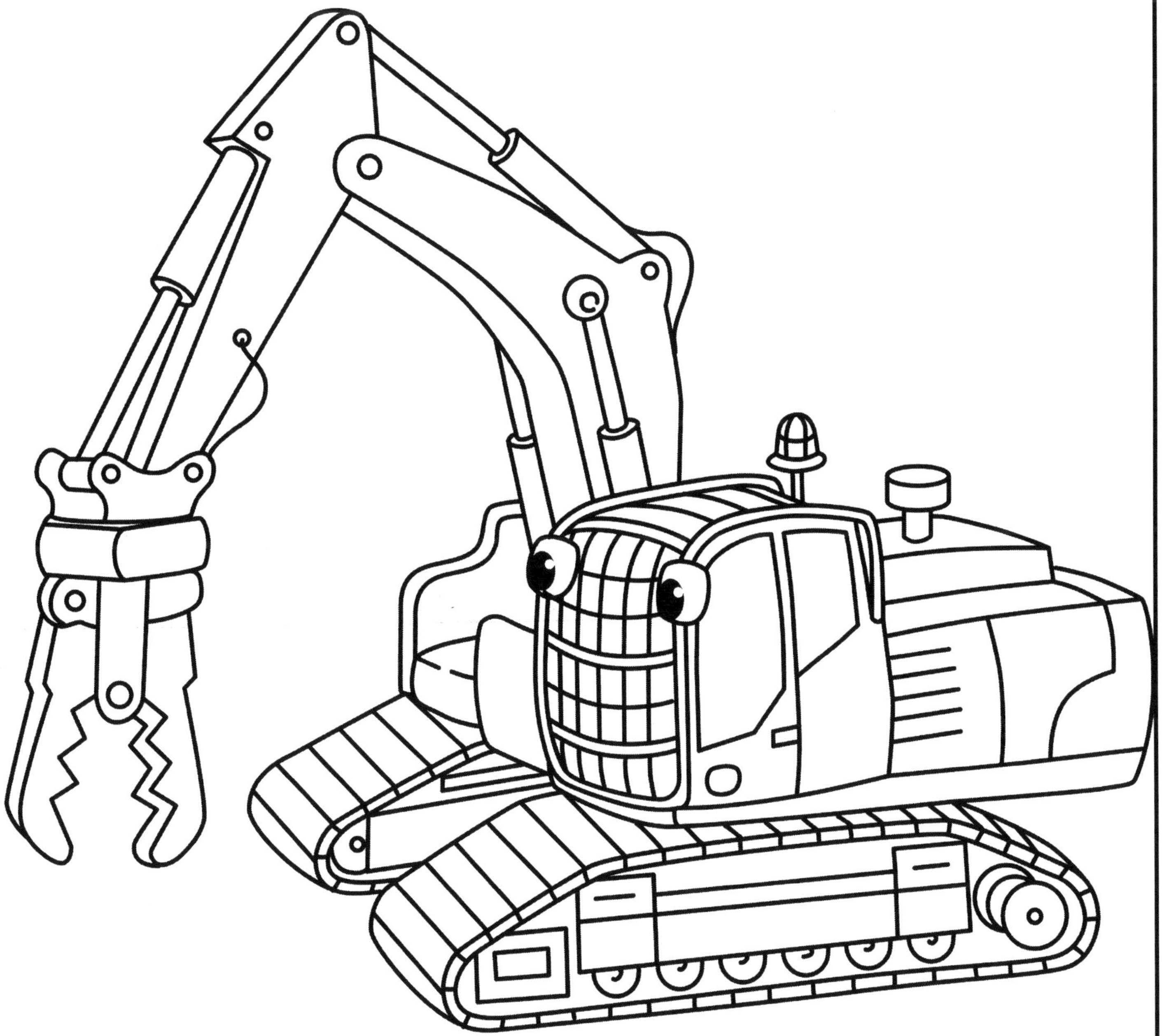

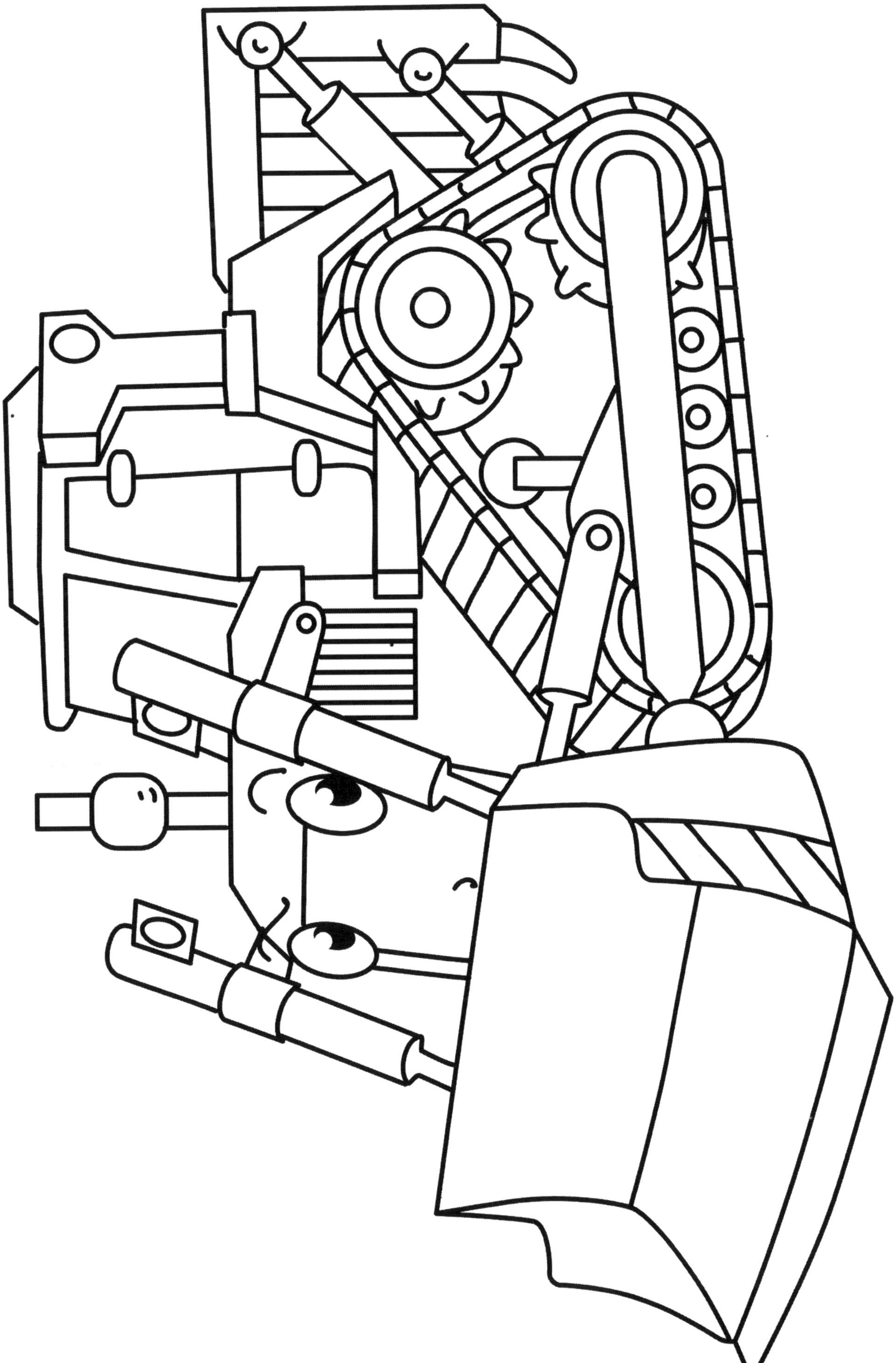

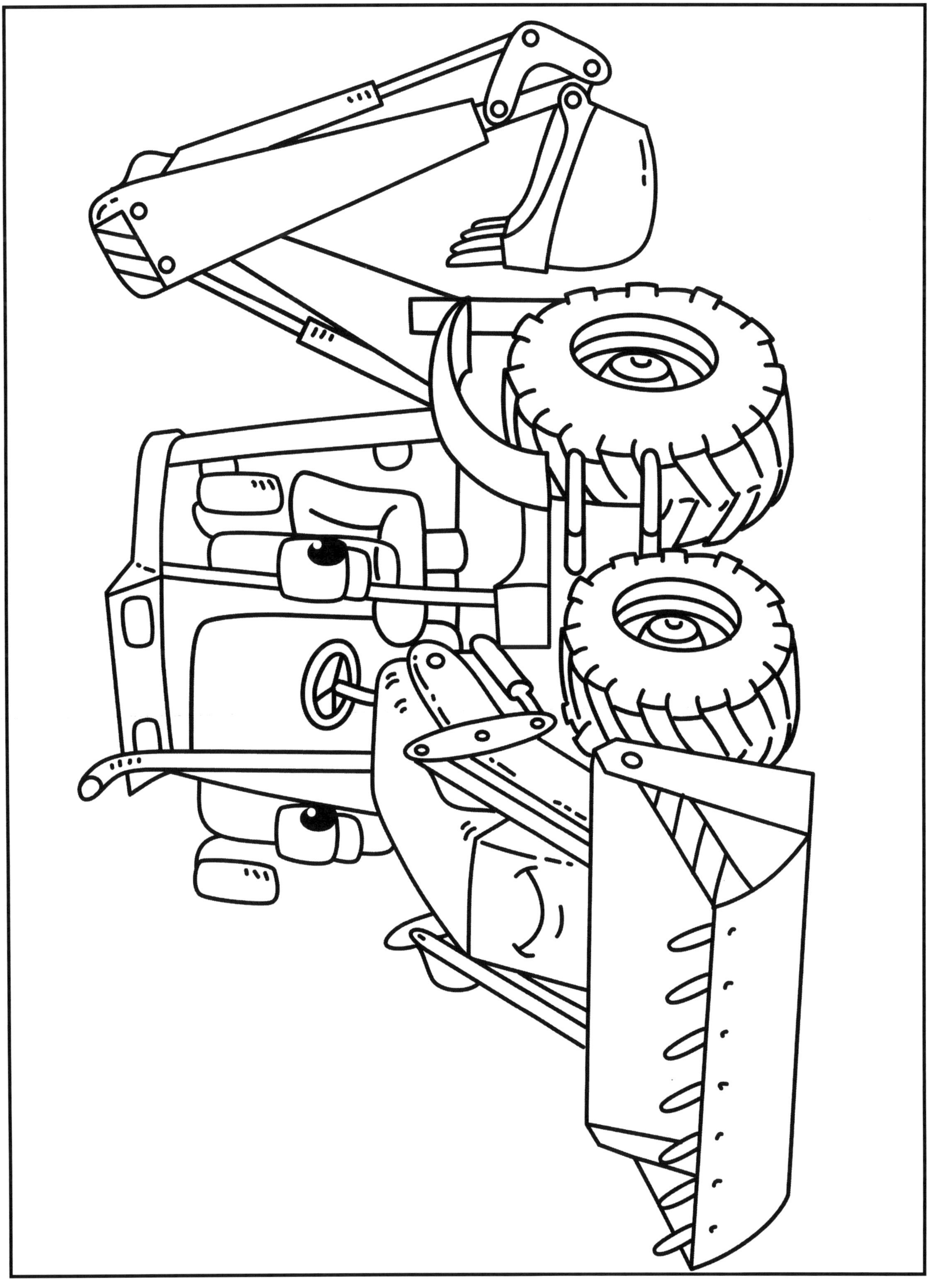

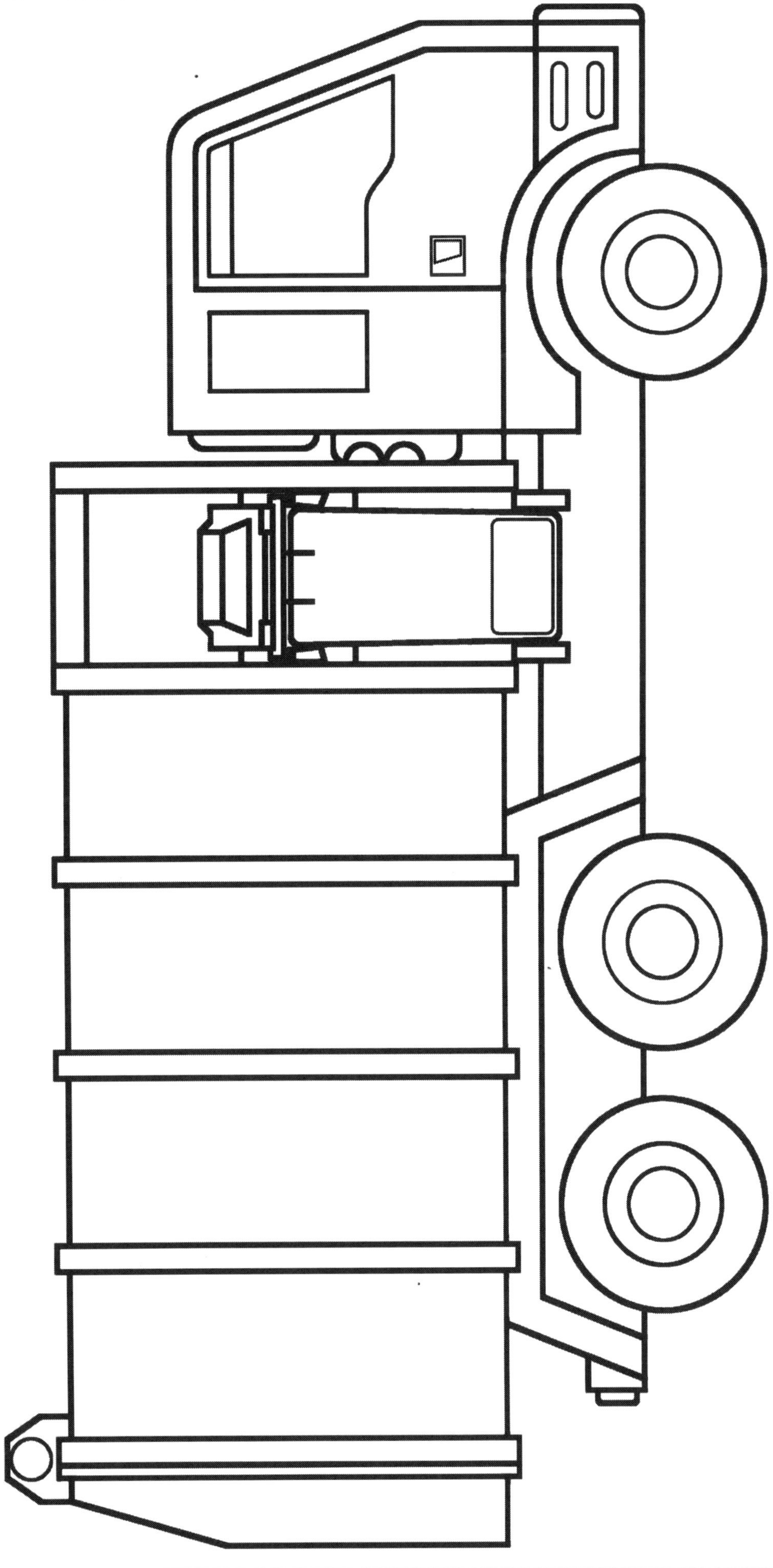

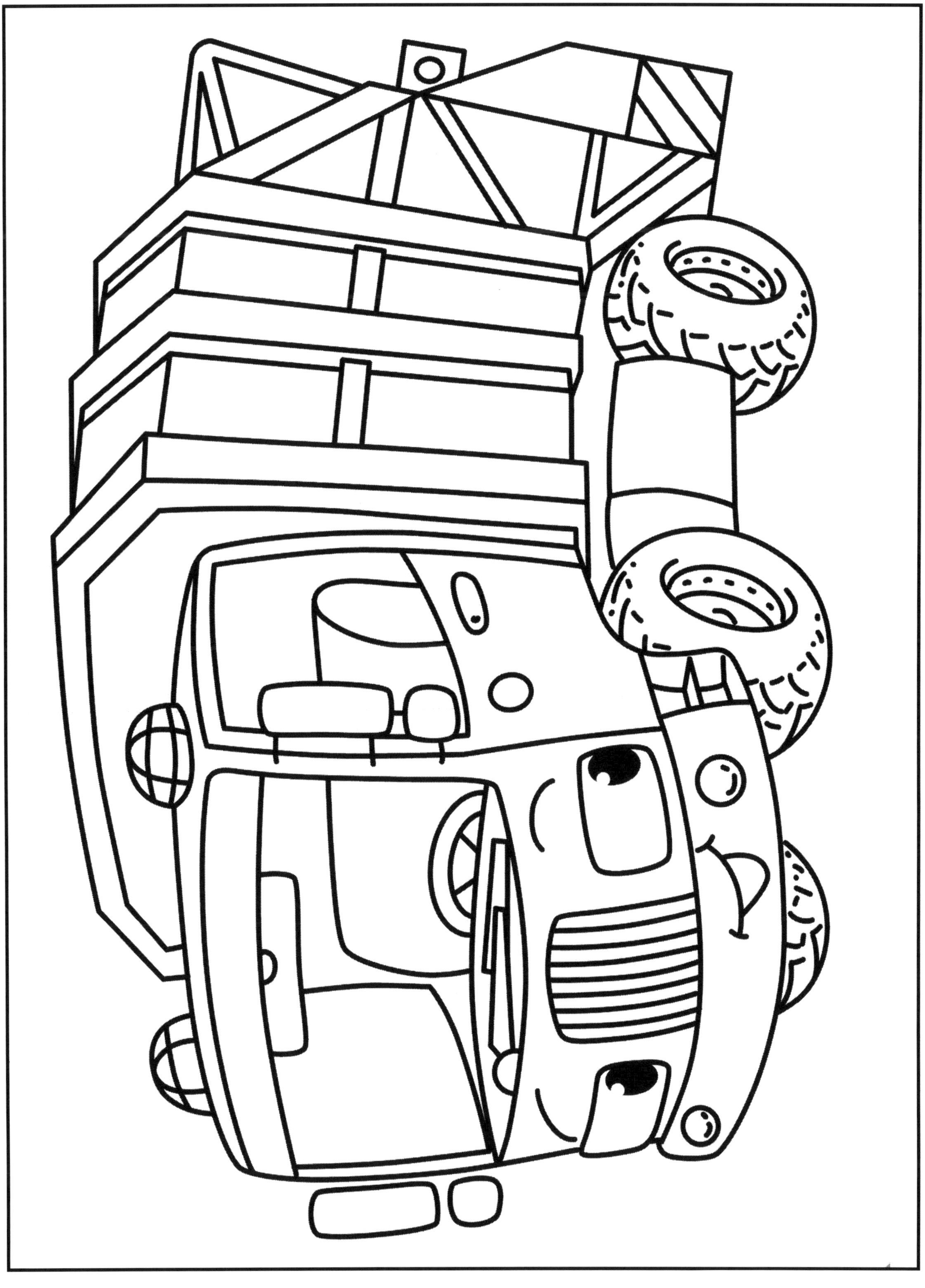

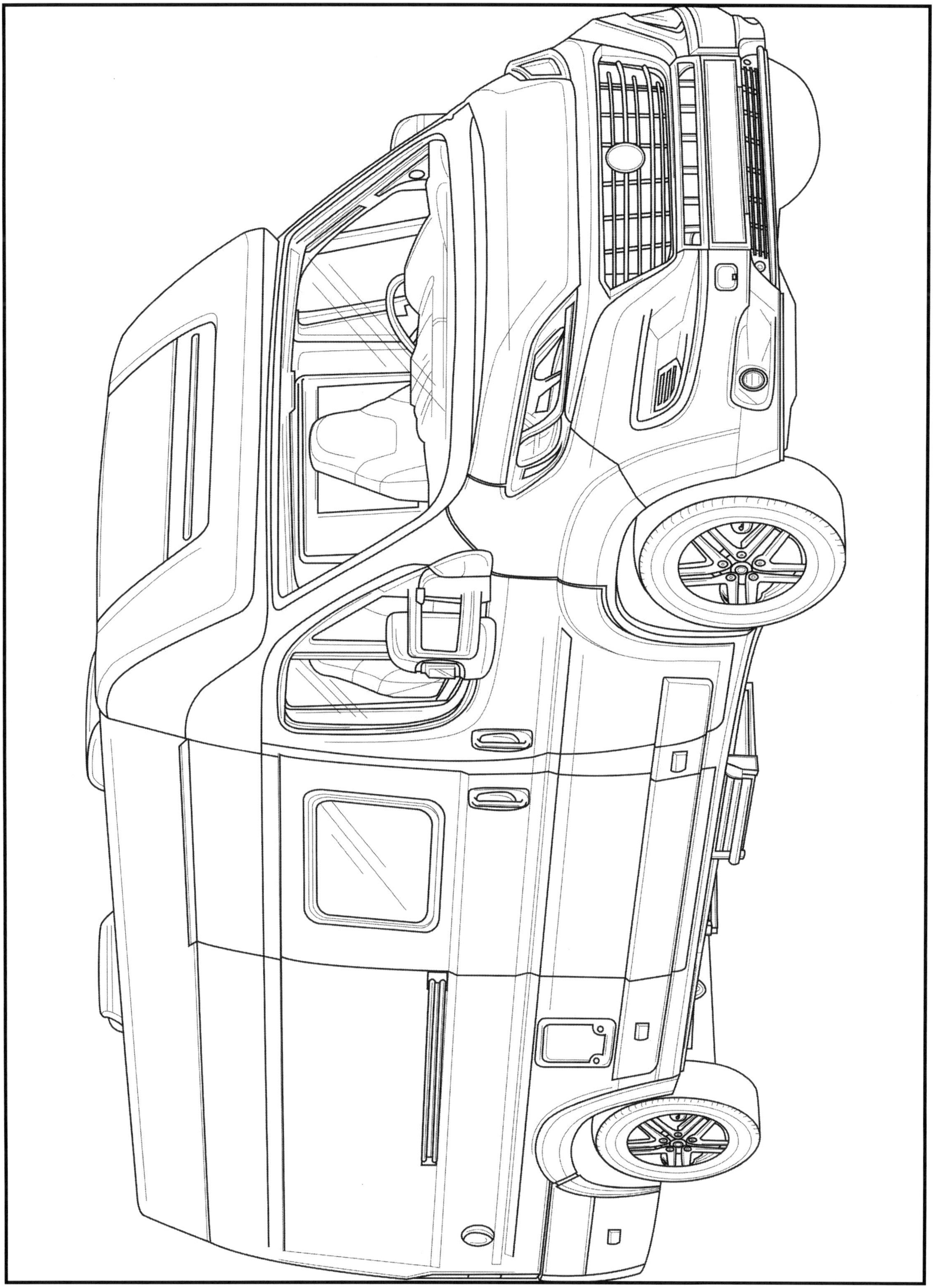

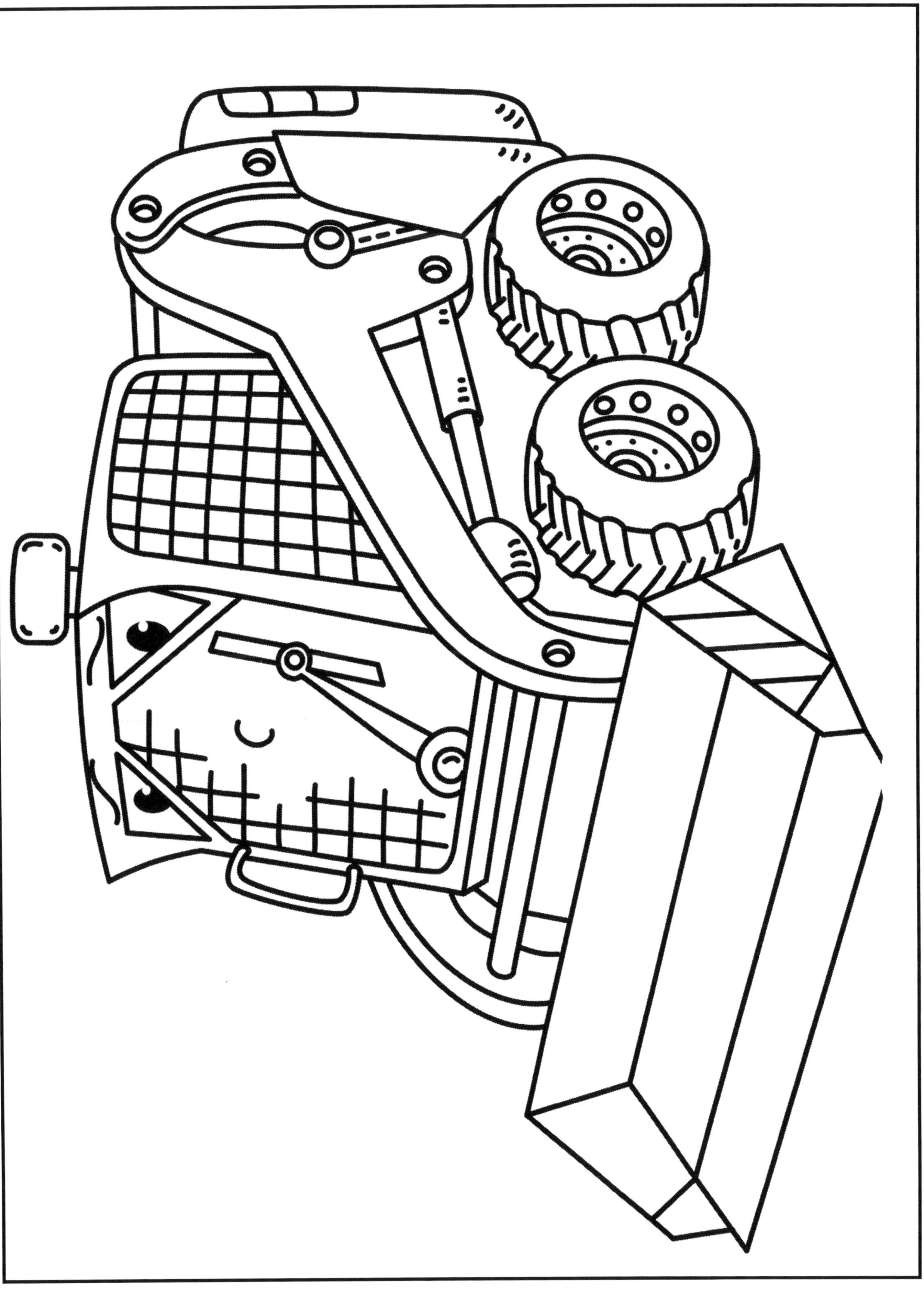

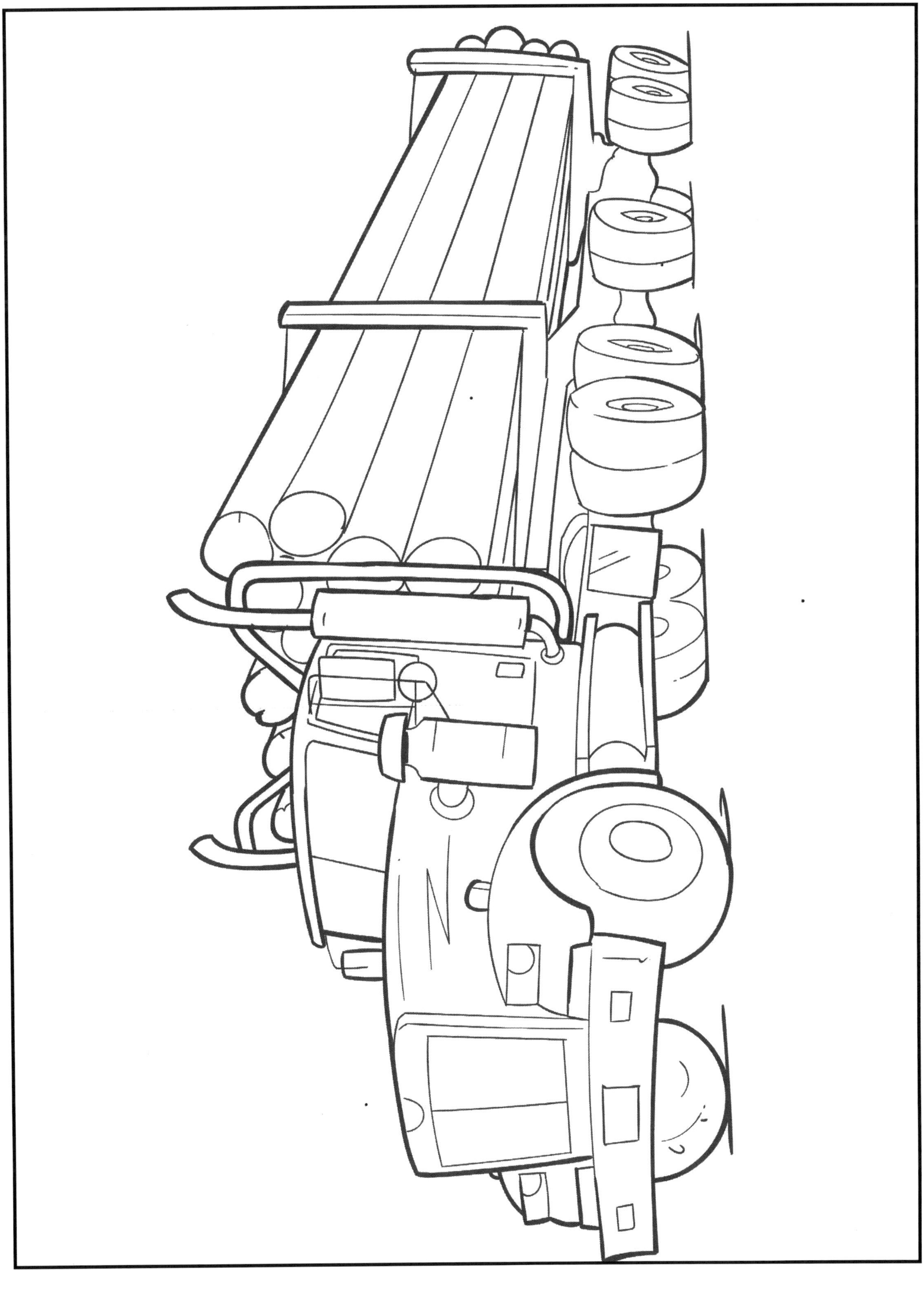

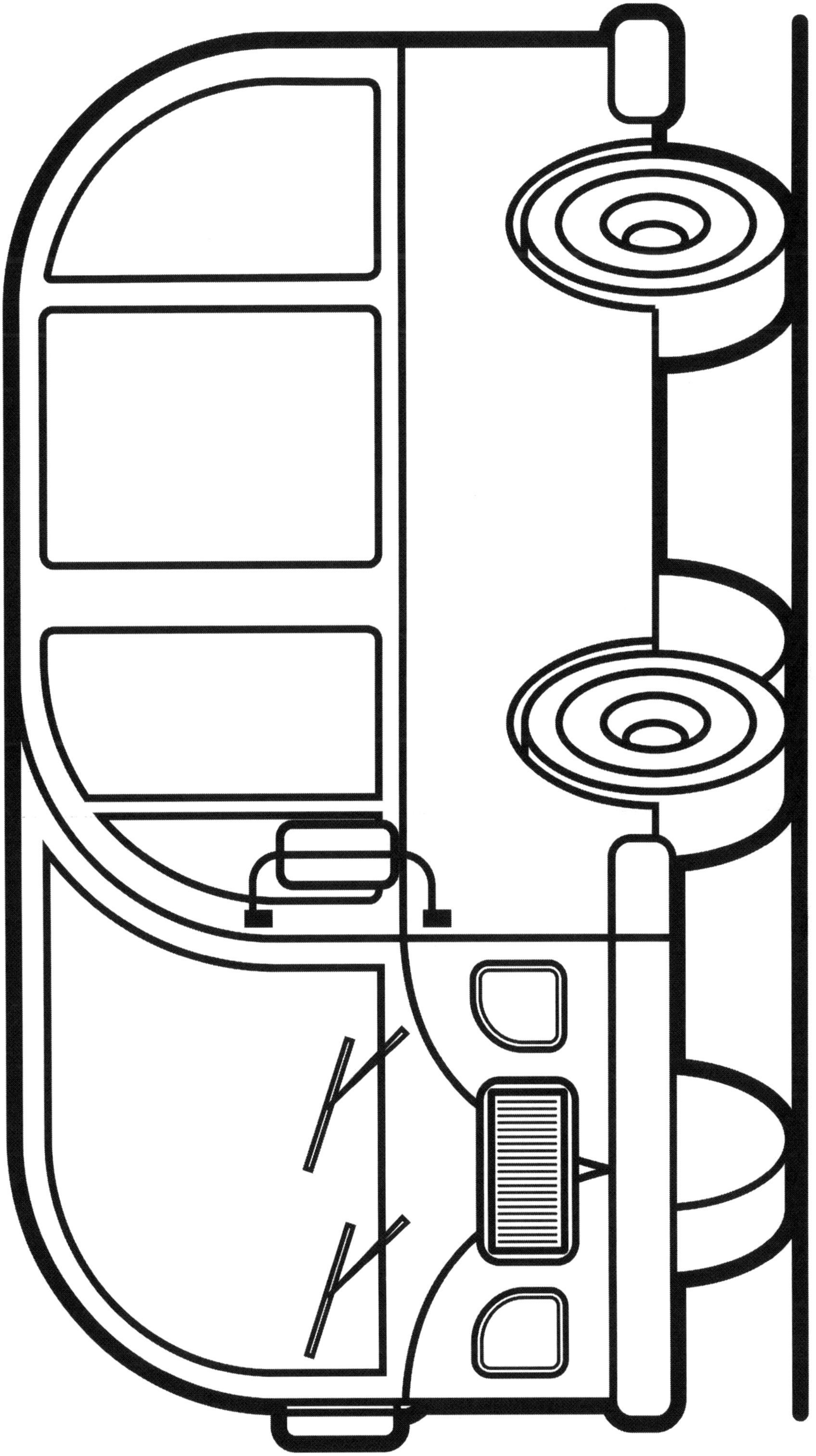

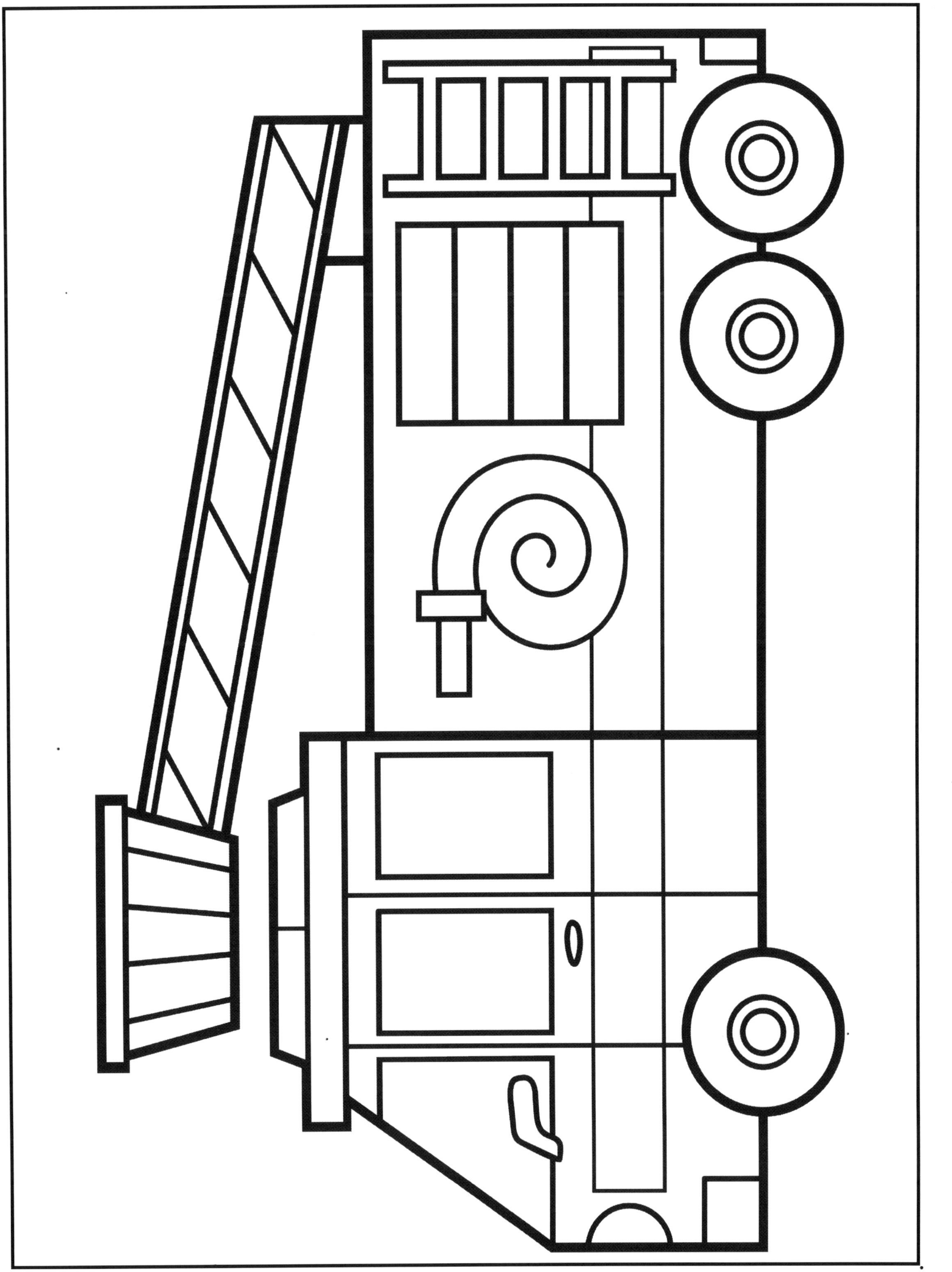

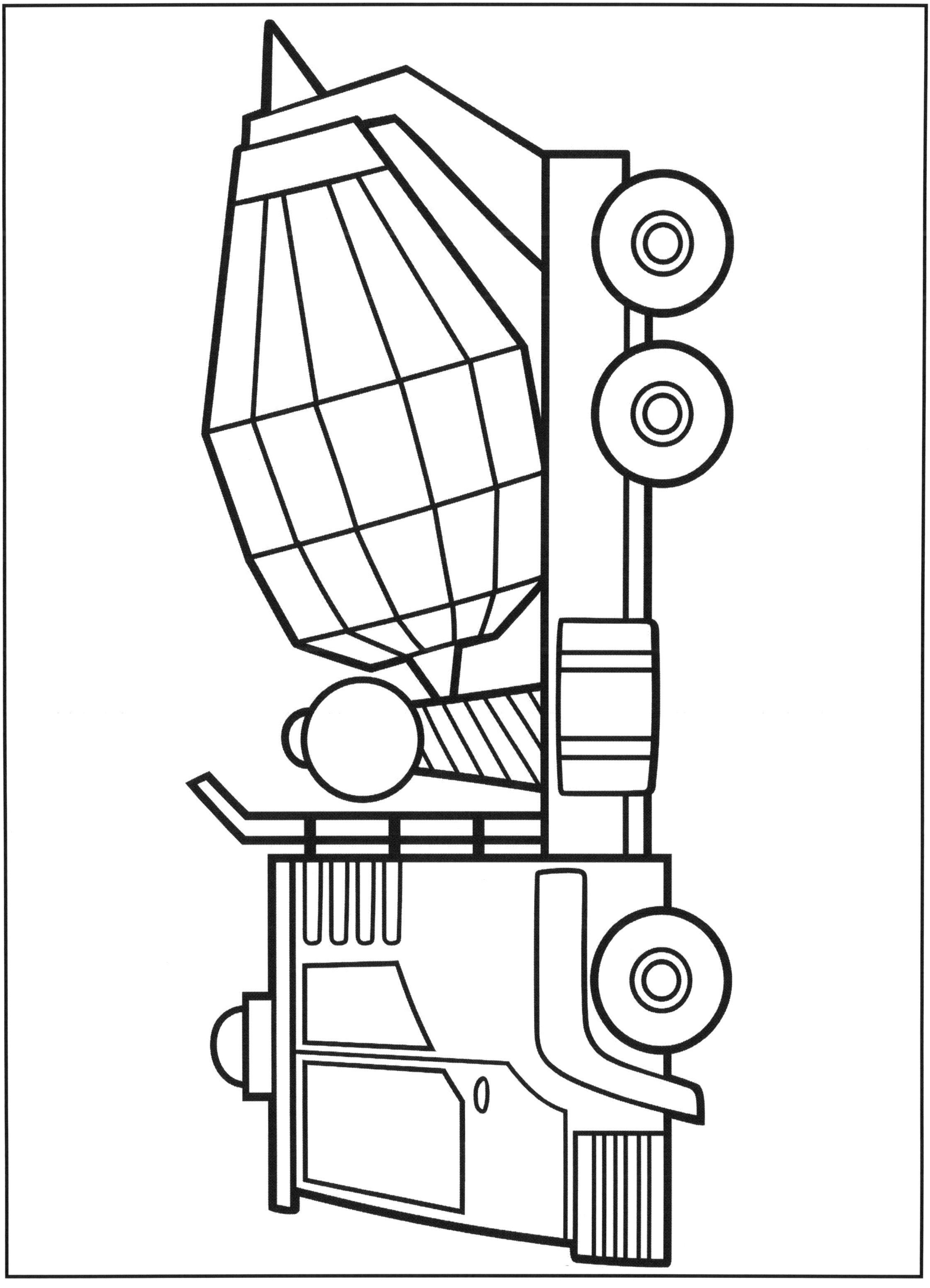

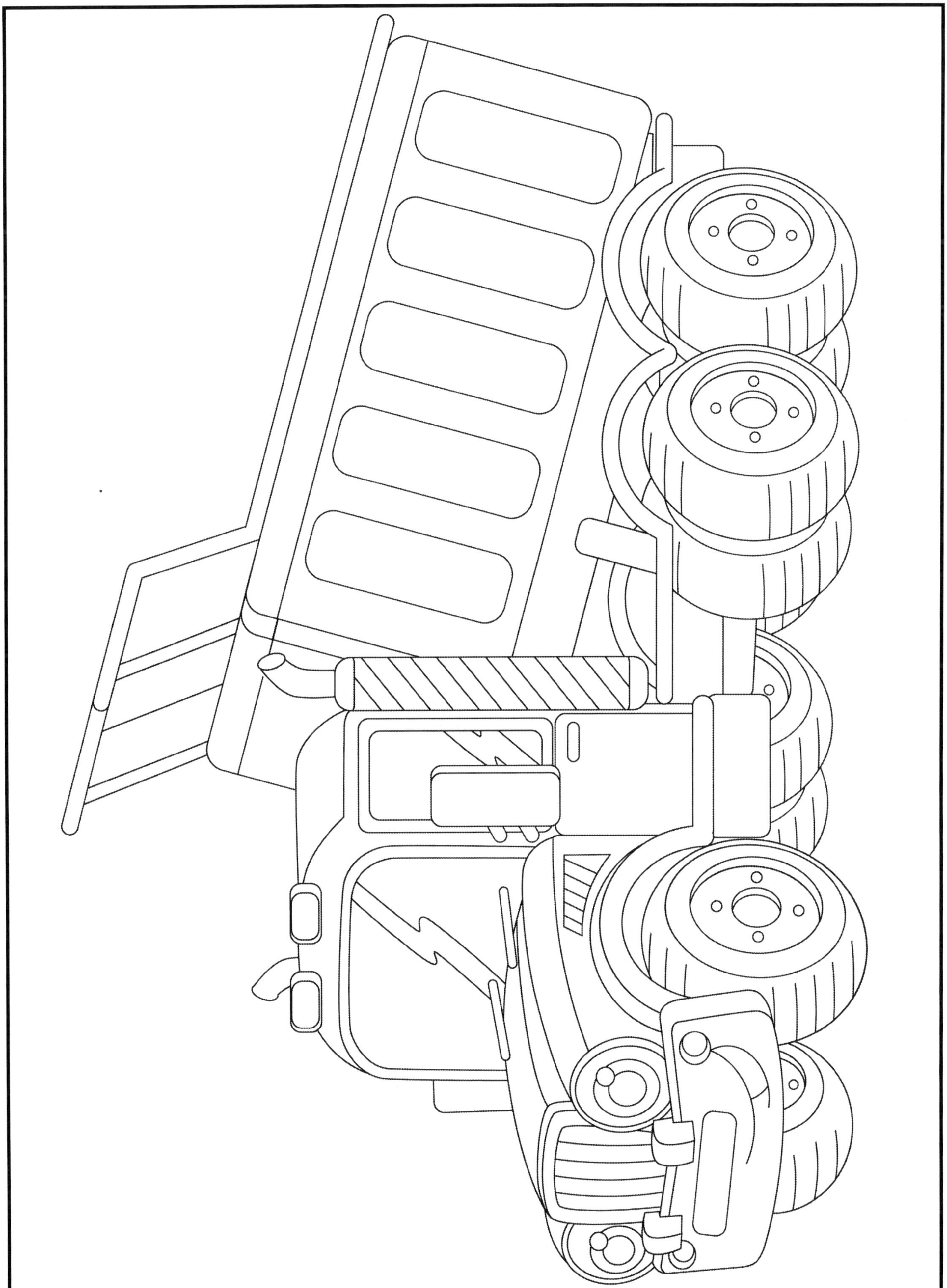

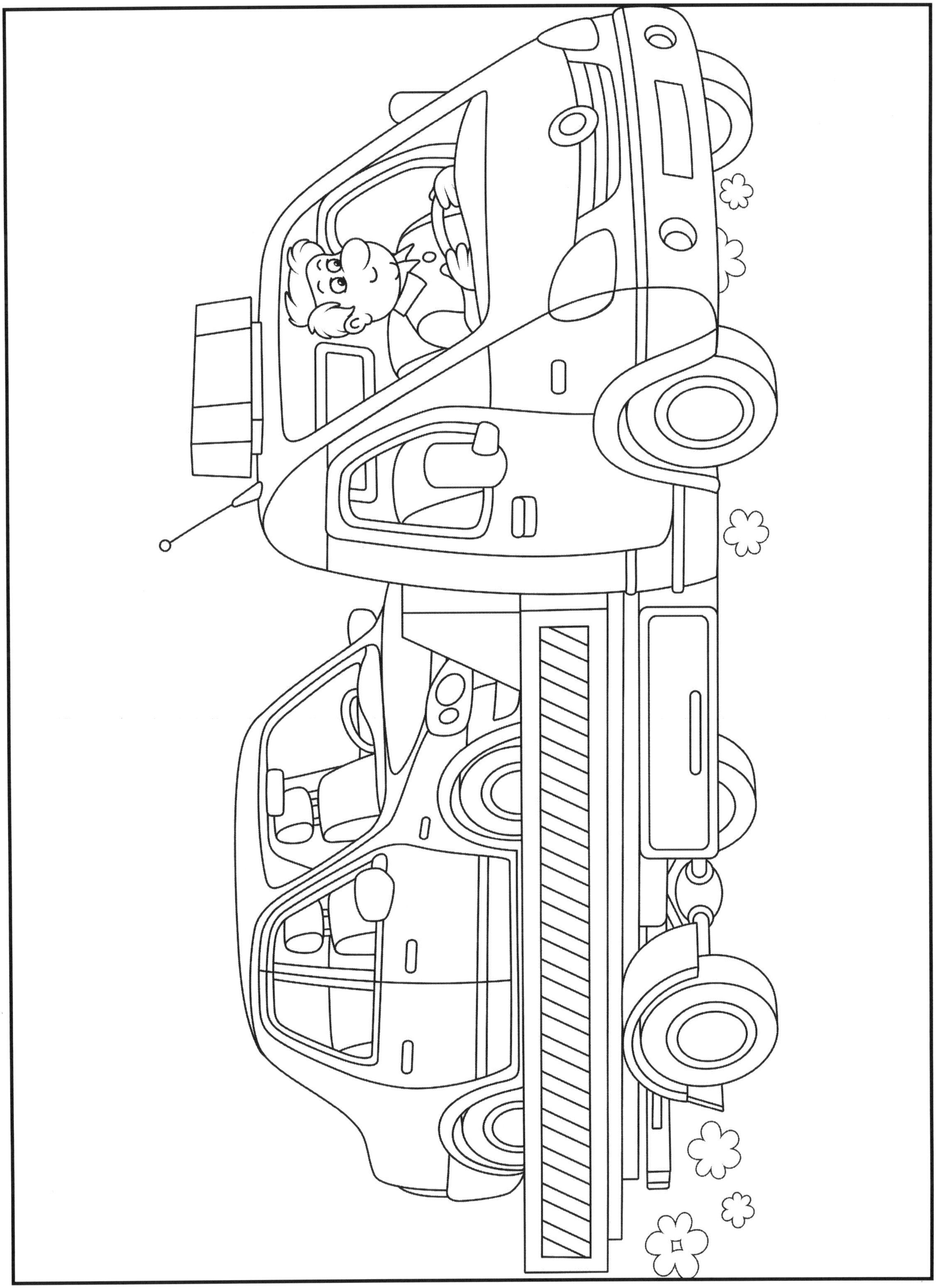

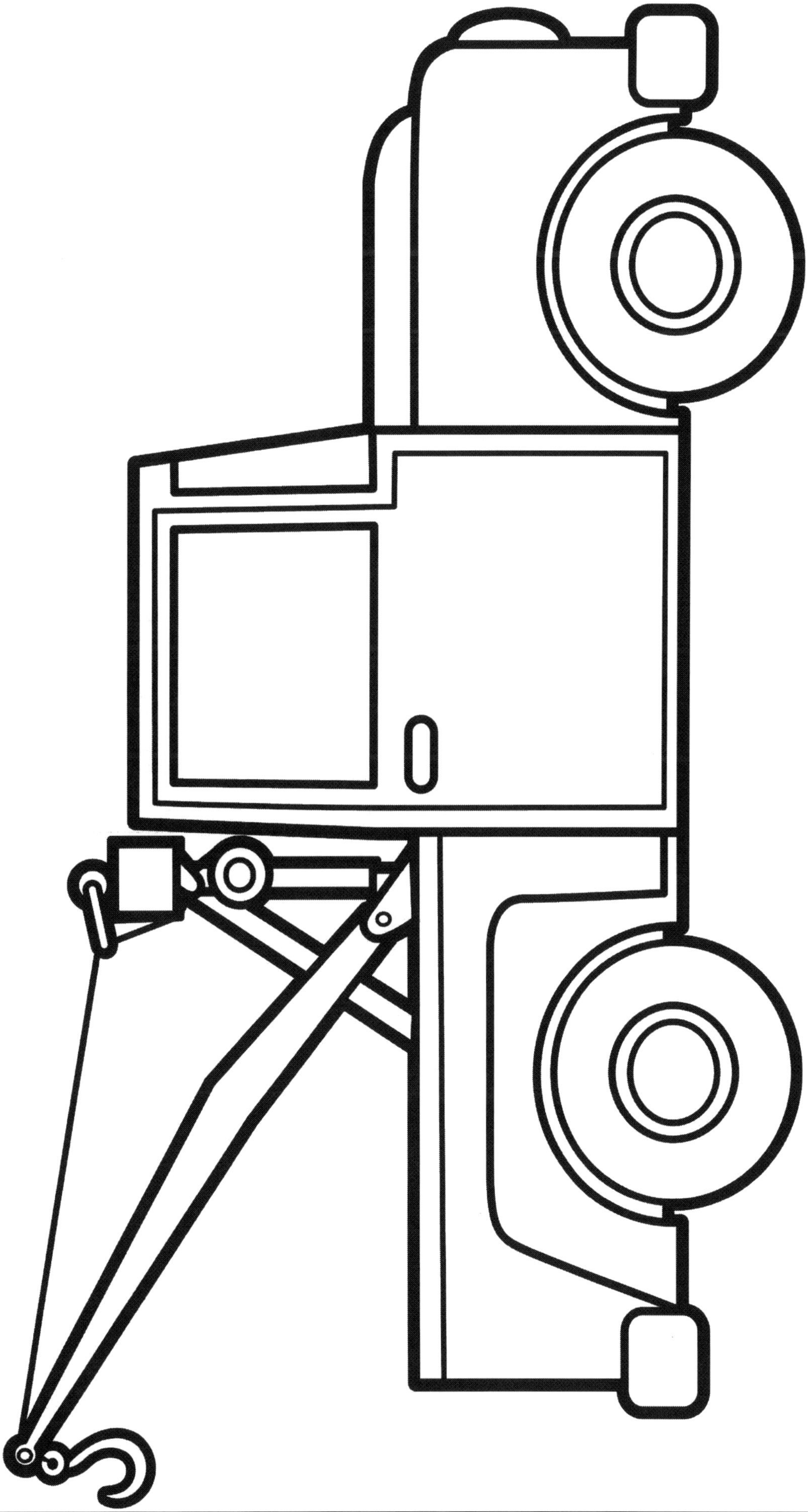

Made in the USA
Columbia, SC
28 June 2022

62407580R00111